Ignite
Your
Psychic
Intuition

About the Author

Teresa Brady, Esquire (Philadelphia, PA) is an attorney in private practice. She is a former professor, head of a business school, and business consultant. Her education includes a BA, MBA, JD, and post-graduate studies at Harvard University. Teresa also holds an honorary doctoral degree. She is a winner of the *Philadelphia Business Journal's* "40 Under 40" award, and is one of the guest hosts of television's *Abington News and Views*.

Teresa has spent decades applying her sixth sense methods. Over the years friends, family, colleagues, and clients from everywhere have sought Teresa out for her wisdom and insight. She always gives encouragement for the future to those who feel discouraged. Visit her online at www.byteresabrady.com and via email at: teresa@byteresabrady.com

Ignite
Your
Psychic
Intuition

An
A to Z Guide
to Developing Your
Sixth Sense

Teresa Brady

Llewellyn Publications
Woodbury, Minnesota

First Edition
First Printing, 2011

Book design by Steffani Sawyer
Book edited by Laura Graves
Cover design by Lisa Novak
Cover Image: iStockphoto.com/Matt Knannlein
Interior artwork © Llewellyn art department

Llewellyn Publications is a registered trademark of Llewellyn Worldwide Ltd.

Library of Congress Cataloging-in-Publication Data
Brady, Teresa, 1956–
  Ignite your psychic intuition: an A to Z guide to developing your sixth sense
/ Teresa Brady. — 1st ed.
    p. cm.
  Includes bibliographical references.
  ISBN 978-0-7387-2170-5
1. Extrasensory perception. 2. Clairvoyance. 3. Intuition—Miscellanea. I.
Title. II. Title: A to Z guide to developing your sixth sense.
  BF1321.B69 2011
  133.8—dc22
                                    2011009252

Llewellyn Publications
A Division of Llewellyn Worldwide Ltd.
2143 Wooddale Drive
Woodbury, MN 55125-2989
www.llewellyn.com

Printed in the United States of America

Acknowledgements

To the late John Joseph Brady and Concetta Teresa Leone-Brady, my dear Dad and Mom—where do I start? Thank you for all you did for me and for all you continue to do for me. Even though you are gone from this world, you are still within me. Thank you for teaching me that whatever happens, good or bad, it all happens for a reason and everything is a blessing. Special thanks to Mom, my teacher and support in my sixth-sense journey. She was a master intuitive.

To Great-Grandpop, Gaetano Leone, who spoke no English but, with his phenomenal sixth sense and expertise in gazing, became a wealthy New Jersey and Pennsylvania entrepreneur and diversified businessman. Your sixth-sense knowledge and practice became the basis and springboard of mine. You clearly proved that the sixth sense is there to bring abundance.

To Aunt Helen and Uncle Jack Kleinhenz, thank you for your kindness and support.

To cousins Joseph and Jan Leone, thank you for all your interest and encouragement with this project, and special thanks to Jan Leone of www.YourLastSite.com for all your work in helping me sort through the complicated and ever-changing online world of marketing. You are truly amazing!

To Robert and Maryann Tinney, thank you for your wonderful friendship. You're not only a great couple but your love for each other radiates to all those you meet. Also, a special "thank you" to Robert's brother, the late Dan Tinney for the honor of knowing you for a short but memorable time.

To Dr. James and Alberta Fiore, thank you for your constant support, enthusiasm, and friendship.

To Angela DeNofa, thank you for your friendship, support, and constant encouragement. You're the best!

To Andrzej and Renata Jadlowski and son Christopher, thank you for all your kindness and wonderful friendship.

To Edward and Lucille Sliwa, thank you for your warmth and wonderful friendship.

To Gordana Chelsvig, phenomenal herbalist, thank you for all the good you do for everyone who crosses your path. Your kindness, thoughtfulness, and friendship are second to none.

To the late Bradford Dooley, thank you for being such a great lifelong friend. I miss you very much.

To former student Daniel Diedrich and new wife, Melissa, Dan, it was an honor to be your teacher and to hear of all the sixth-sense help you received when you were in that horrific accident and during your long, intense recovery.

To Carrie Obry, Amy Glaser, Laura Graves, and everyone at Llewellyn who worked so hard on this project, thank you very much.

To Paula Brancato, poet, filmmaker, professor, moderator of the *Poets and Writers* interest group at the Harvard Club of NYC, thank you for your excellent advice and constant availability.

To Lisa Scottoline, thank you for giving me and everyone who crosses your path the direction, encouragement, and enthusiasm to take a manuscript and convert it into a book.

Sometimes people come into our lives very briefly but their presence is exactly what we need at that moment. Sometimes they can even change our destiny. That is the case with Barry Goldin, Esq., without whose excellent advice and counsel this project may not have come to fruition. He is truly what a lawyer was meant to be in every sense of the word.

To Master Park, thank you for sharing your genius for healing. You never cease to amaze me.

To Roz Fulton of "Direction and Exposure," thank you for developing the actress in me.

To Anna Smith, thank you for all you do. You are a great person and wonderful secretary.

To the celebrities from all walks of life whose lives act as my inspiration, including David Foster, M. Knight Shamalyan, Oprah Winfrey, and Andrew Lloyd Webber. I enjoy watching your genius at work as it continues to blossom. Don't forget, lots of sixth-sense information has helped make you who you are.

To all those highly elevated souls, here or who have passed, who act not only as my inspiration but also as my mentors and heroes, Dannion Brinkley, Sylvia Browne, Edgar Cayce, Jeane Dixon, and Phil Jordan. Your lives and stories are amazing.

Above all a special "thank you" to Bella, "the Belle," my faithful writing assistant, who never left my side during those many long hours of writing and revising. Your only reward was a small cat treat. How I wish I had your patience and simplicity of spirit.

To my Dad and Mom–

Thank you for everything

Contents

Introduction:
Tune In to Your Higher Power

It's shocking to think that most people struggle to make good things happen in their lives with few positive outcomes; all they have to do is tap into their powerful psychic intuition, creating the life they want and the happiness they deserve.

You can learn to ignite your own psychic intuition and reap all the rewards a charmed life has to offer. You alone hold the key to opening the door to your higher senses and transforming yourself from being a passive spectator and receiver of what life throws at you, to becoming a pro-active mover and shaker in the creation of your own destiny. How can you do this? By applying the twenty-six tools I share with you in this book.

Ignite Your Psychic Intuition: An A-Z Guide to Developing Your Sixth Sense brings the dynamic, transformative potential of heightened senses to anyone who cares to develop these skills. It contains all the information, exercises, and tools you'll need to tune into the world in a way you may have never before. The results are positive and life changing.

Simply put, this book takes our ordinary alphabet and repurposes each letter as a psychic development tool, allowing you to quickly and naturally advance your sixth sense abilities. Think of this book as your personal "how to" reference handbook and support system all in one, with step-by-step explanations of how to develop your sixth sense in a totally new way. By following the techniques within, you can open yourself to an exciting new level of consciousness. You will see the unseen, hear the inaudible, sense the intangible, and know what is not apparently evident when you become "sixth-sense-sensitive"—that is, you will tap into universal energy for the sole purpose of having a better life.

Some people think being psychic or intuitive is best left to the well-known television personalities or the "local psychic" whose information can at times dazzle and overload a client or audience with everyday facts about a lost loved one. Sixth sense experiences presented to you in this way may not necessarily improve your life—you already know your lost loved one's hair color or favorite dessert. Although the information is well-intentioned and may give some comfort to those of us left behind, this book takes spiritual information and makes it more productive and conducive to positive action. Put the control and outcome of your life and the comfort of true sixth sense knowledge where it should be, with you. Begin today to be the proactive one to make the doors swing open, allowing synchronicity to begin. You are the one who makes this happen *by* yourself and *for* yourself through my twenty-six tools.

As you use the tools in this book, keep in mind that there is nothing magical or unusual about having heightened senses. On the contrary, perceptions through heightened senses are very real and can come as easily as perceptions through the ordinary senses. In fact, heightening your sixth sense is one of the greatest gifts you can cultivate. When you think about it, most of what we do is based on the unseen and intangible. For example, we think, speak, hear, and experience all kinds of positive and negative emotions and feelings. What I propose in this book is simply adding the spiritual component to what we already naturally perceive all the time.

This book is for everyone. If you are a novice just beginning the higher sense journey, I will walk you through the process of opening your senses and provide confidence that what you are sensing is indeed real. For you veterans of sixth sense development, you will enjoy the stories, examples, additional tools, and maybe a different perspective to add to your practice of heightening the senses.

Your past and present relationships will noticeably improve once you've added the sixth sense component to your life. You will make better decisions and give better advice to loved ones and close friends. For those of you looking for romance, adding the sixth sense makes you wiser in your romantic choices.

Whatever your job or station in life, having a well-developed sixth sense will help you be better at what you do. In any career you can imagine, developing your sixth sense will open the door to more inspiration and creativity. As for me, I am an attorney practicing law in a large metropolitan city, a traditional field where one wouldn't normally expect to find someone who conscientiously develops their higher senses. But I have found my sixth sense plays a vital role in my everyday life as a lawyer. My heightened senses help me push past the perceived barriers and better assist those who call on me for help. Over the years, I've collected so many tips for developing the sixth sense that I decided I *had* to share them. I love working with these tools because they come so naturally and their benefits are too good to miss. Once you learn how to tune in to your higher power, you will reap rewards in all areas of your life. I truly hope that my methods will open you to having a happier and more satisfying life.

Part I sets the groundwork, defining what the sixth sense is. I use everyday examples to illustrate how to simply take the basic human senses and develop them to a higher, more advanced level. Part II is composed of my step-by-step method of naturally developing your sixth sense. I use each letter of the alphabet as the base because I believe the alphabet is an excellent mnemonic tool, allowing for easy recall of concepts and examples even years after reading this book.

Some wonder if the tools as presented here will take many months or years to see results. The answer to that is a solid *no*. From the moment you begin to read this book, you will view life differently and open yourself up to what may not be readily apparent. You will instantly become aware of a higher consciousness in and around you. Following the tools outlined in this book will become a natural part of your schedule. As you practice my methods, sixth sense development will become part of your lifestyle, and more importantly, part of your true essence. Be creative, explore the tools, have fun applying them, but most of all, make this book your constant companion. Keep it with you and view it as your loving support system instructing, guiding, and cheering you on as you embark on your sixth sense journey.

PART I

A Detailed Look at the Powerful Sixth Sense

Before we can turn to the tools in the A-to-Z portion of the book, this part of the book will act as an introduction to a number of concepts that will empower you to get the most out of the time and effort you expend on developing your sixth sense. I consider this part not only a sixth sense overview, but also an insightful chapter where you can focus your efforts to begin an advanced program of spiritual development. Read this section with an open mind toward sixth sense enlightenment. Take each of the concepts and examples I provide and use them as a springboard for recollecting your own encounters with the sixth sense. Think about how your experiences affected spiritual development throughout your life. Have these experiences made you a wiser, better person for having them? Were they spiritual and profound? Some people's personalities transform completely after experiencing a major sixth sense event. Sometimes a life-focus-readjustment can take place whereby one's view of life changes from focusing on mundane pettiness to viewing all of life as truly profound. Whatever the result, the changes to one's life are almost always positive, creating a more grounded and peaceful personality.

Let us now start at the very foundation of what the sixth sense is. For our purposes, the sixth sense takes the basic human senses and adds a spiritual or mystical component connecting us to that which is bigger or greater than what we perceive through our ordinary senses. The sixth sense makes itself known through the unexplained visuals, sounds, knowledge, nudges, and/or feelings that enter through your senses and act as alerts to the good or bad that is soon to enter your life. The sixth sense allows you to see, hear, taste, feel, and smell what may not be apparent through your other senses, but its existence is very real.

Let's take the example of the gut feeling. What does the sudden bad gut feeling you get when you meet one person signify, as opposed to the significance of an instantaneous feeling of a leaping heart when you meet another? In each example is an important sixth sense message. You just need to more systematically develop your senses to have more of these moments of sixth sense encounters, and you need to be able to instantaneously interpret them so you are guarded and guided throughout your life.

Although the mechanics of the sixth sense may sound complicated, you don't have to be so concerned about how it works. You just have to be the grateful recipient of its love, wisdom, and knowledge.

By being aware of your sixth sense, spiritual guidance and comfort are yours just for the asking. You may not realize it, but in the course of a typical day, the number of sixth sense messages trying to make their way through to you is infinite. From this moment forward, pay close attention to the sixth sense information that flows through you on a regular day. When something just comes to you, stop to think about what it is. Take time to decipher the purpose of the information trying to come through. In addition, be aware that the same information can come to you through more than one sense. I refer to this overlap of sensory information as "sixth sense overlap." Take special notice when sixth sense overlap occurs. If a message is trying to get your attention by coming through more than one sense, it is very important. It is either an alert to seize a valuable opportunity or a major warning to refrain from action. For example, when the messages come, you may receive a clairvoyant or visual image accompanied by a strongly negative "gut" feeling. To illustrate the sixth sense overlap, let's assume you are thinking of driving to a friend's house very late and you get an instantaneous visual image of an ambulance accompanied by a bad gut feeling. Your sixth sense may be warning you about a possible automobile accident. Whether you receive a single sixth sense message or multiple messages, and whether the messages are positive or negative, welcome them and act on them. The free flow of sixth sense information is a positive sign of your spiritual development.

We are now ready for a detailed look at our human senses on a higher level. Our focus will be on seeing, hearing, knowing, feeling, touch, smelling and tasting. There are actually more, but these are the basics and they will be our center of attention. In addition, some authors may categorize the senses somewhat differently. It all works out to be the same. Following are some examples of clairvoyance, clairaudience, claircognizance, and more.

Clairvoyance: Clear Sight

Clairvoyance, also known as "clear seeing," is the ability to psychically see what is not apparent to regular human sight. There are normally two ways a person can see clairvoyantly. The clairvoyant may see the physical world and the nonphysical world side by side. The physical world looks "solid," while the nonphysical is more transparent or translucent. Much more common is the ability to see through the third eye. Third eye sight is an interesting phenomenon because it is believed that eons ago, a third eye physically existed on humans. The third eye is said to have been located in the upper mid-section of the forehead. On yourself, you can easily find the position of the third eye. Just take the tip of your index finger and touch the center of your forehead. You will intuitively touch the third eye spot, the place on the middle of the forehead that feels slightly empty, as if something used to fill its place.

I am acquainted with many energy workers who claim the term "third eye" is actually a misnomer. They maintain the "third eye" should be called the "first eye" because it was believed to be our true, original method of sight. The third eye is still considered to be the soul's gateway to see past the veil, which is the barrier separating our world (the third dimension) from the world of higher vibration commonly known as the fourth dimension.

It is very important to remember that spiritual vision through the third eye has nothing to do with physical vision. You can be blind and have a well-developed third eye that allows you to see clairvoyantly. You can experience third eye vision from the top, front, sides, and back of the head; or when your eyes are open, closed, looking up, or looking down.

Many who aren't familiar with mystical concepts stubbornly and erroneously believe it is impossible to see images through the third eye. On the contrary, seeing through the third eye is actually very easy to do. Try this—close your eyes, and take a moment to imagine the face of your favorite person. If you can picture your favorite person in your mind, you are using your third eye. The only difference from ordinary sight is that the act of imagining the person was what you directed. When you see clairvoyantly through your third eye, the opposite action takes place. The universal consciousness sends images to you. Since you have no control over the spiritual images sent to you, pay attention. These messages are important, accurate, reliable, useful, and most of all, pertinent to your life.

Now, let's take a look at how visual images are clairvoyantly transmitted to you. The method of image transmittal can occur in different ways. Some images may be transmitted very slowly, some very quickly, and others may be transmitted as still shots unfolding like a picture book. Other images may be transmitted similar to a movie, flowing along in a continuous storytelling fashion. Oftentimes the image transmitted to you is a single one with nothing preceding and nothing following. The images can be in color, black and white, shades of gray, or some combination. Clairvoyant images can be of people, animals, places, or things. Words, letters, numbers, colors, and symbols can also be seen clairvoyantly. In addition, the images can be literal or symbolic in meaning.

Having clairvoyant ability does not mean you can see the past, present, and future. Some clairvoyants can only perceive images that pertain to the present, and not the past or future. I refer to them as limited clairvoyants. The images they see are presently relevant. If a limited clairvoyant sees a brick house positioned near you, that house is probably the house you live in, and not the one you'll buy next year. This type of clairvoyant ability is useful for confirming what's already evident, but it really needs to be developed to be useful. Limited clairvoyant ability is not the focus of this book. The purpose here is to make you an expansive clairvoyant, one who can break through the time barrier to see the past and the future.

Let's begin with timing. It takes lots of practice to determine if what you are seeing is a past, future, or presently occurring event. To do so, you'll need a keen thought process (itself a product of practice and verification), and of course, don't forget your common sense.

Timing seems to be a true individual ability. Although your method may be different, let me explain how I see timing—in image position and color—to get you started. Let's start with position. If the images are parallel to the person, it is a present event. If the image is just slightly in front of the person, the event will occur in the near future. If the image appears further in front of the person, the event may occur within a few years. The opposite evidences a past event. If the image is directly behind the person, it pertains to the near past, but if positioned farther behind them, the event occurred in the distant past. Anything positioned in between is just that.

Now let's look at color to determine timing. Again, your method may be different, but here is how color relates to timing for me. Bright clear colors mean the present or future, with variations within them. I perceive gray as the color of the past. A lighter gray is a near past event and a very dark shade of gray is the very distant past, perhaps an event occurring decades earlier. For timing in between the two, the image is presented in shades of medium gray with many variations in hue. As for very distant future images, I frown on paying too much attention to them as there are so many life variables along with free will that can change that event from occurring. I never want anyone to sit back and wait for either a good or bad event to happen.

I believe refining the timing of an event is a challenge that will keep you on your toes, but you'll soon figure it out. Along with the importance of refining an event's timing is symbol interpretation, which also takes practice. I suggest you begin to keep a list of the clairvoyant symbols you've encountered and your interpretation of them. Your list will become your personal dictionary to be added to and referred to often. (See the chapter, "Keep Journals.") As you build your dictionary, you will become increasingly accurate in symbol interpretation. Refer to and rely on your dictionary whenever you attempt to interpret visuals. Obviously, you will be stumped from time to time. When this happens, do your best and maintain your patience. The meaning of a symbol will become clear in its own time and manner. As an example, let's assume you see the instantaneous image of small bright stars sitting on top a person's shoulders. What could that image mean? Within a split second you should connect the meaning of the burst of light from bright stars to something positive, such as happy events coming or good surprises. Also look at the stars' position—sitting on top of the person's shoulders. This means the good surprises are about to manifest. The brighter and closer the stars are to the body, the sooner the surprises will come. The larger they are, the greater the surprise or happiness. Let's now focus on the following clairvoyant examples offered to spark your thinking about how common and natural clairvoyance is in our lives.

The Symbol: ◊

Every day for two years before I opened my second law office location, I kept receiving the following clairvoyant image: ◊. The image made no sense to me, but I knew it was important. Whatever ◊ meant, I had a good feeling about it. No harm or danger was present, but it took over two years for me to understand the symbol's significance.

Two years to the day of receiving the visual image, I visited the building that was to become my new law office. The ◊ symbol was the repeated pattern in the tile on the entire first floor! When I saw it, I was stunned and felt an immediate déjà vu moment. The mystery was finally solved. Along with all my factual due diligence about the property itself and its location, I had no second thoughts or doubts of any kind. I knew purchasing this property would be an excellent decision. I did purchase the building and it has been one of the wisest business decisions I've ever made.

Keep in mind that once the riddle of a clairvoyant visual is solved, the clairvoyant message stops. In my example, once I made the connection to the ◊ symbol, I never saw it clairvoyantly again. At the moment the connection is made, the universal consciousness has completed its work and it's now time for the recipient of the message—in this case, me—to make a decision. I had the free will to purchase the property or walk away; it was my choice. In this case I chose to buy and from that purchase, many good things have come to me.

Mary and the Red Rose

Let's take another example of a clairvoyant message. Assume you receive a clairvoyant image of a red rose encased in a clear heart above one shoulder of your sister, whom we'll call "Mary." Mary has been experiencing unrequited love for many years. You happily interpret the red rose as a symbol of true love that will come in the future. You roughly determine the timing of love's arrival by focusing on the condition of the rose and its proximity to Mary. You notice the rose is in full bloom and is positioned very close to Mary, which signals that love may arrive very soon. On the contrary, if the rose were a bud and positioned further away, there may be some waiting to do before Mary and her mate come together. In addition, the meaning of the clear heart in which the rose is encased is also significant. Its clarity tells you Mary will be in a very loving, healthy relationship, one certainly worth the wait.

Let's change gears and look at the following more serious examples. I offer them because not all of what you see is sweet and nice. Some images will be negative. The two examples below come directly from my law practice, so if you enjoy sixth sense development and stories about the law, you're in for a double treat! As you might imagine, I get quite a sixth sense workout in my law office. The following examples are not as delightful as Mary's story and my seeing the symbol, but they're great for illustrative purposes.

Handcuffs, Prison Cell, and a Dead Body

Mel came to me for a serious legal matter. Part of the discussion focused on whether he had ever served jail time. As Mel emphatically replied, "No, never," a startling image of handcuffs, a prison cell, and a dead body appeared above his left shoulder. When I questioned Mel further, he admitted he did do jail time several years ago for a gang murder, but he didn't think his record had any relevance to the present criminal charges. His reason for concealing the truth made no sense—he should have realized that I would uncover all the facts sooner rather than later. In this case, the crime and the punishment were literally written all over him.

Child Support, Who Me?

A few years ago, a man named Terry came into my office for an emergency legal matter. I knew this was going to be an interesting case because as he sat down, his visual story unfolded. Dark gray images of several children of various ages and sizes could be seen behind both his shoulders. It was interesting to see that next to each child was a very large dollar symbol, $. The visual image immediately led me to believe Terry owed not only numerous past child support payments, but these amounts were large. How did I know the debt was an old one? The darker gray images of children were the clue.

I began to ask Terry specifically if he owed any domestic support obligations. He looked at the floor and insistently replied, "No." Throughout the interview, Terry consistently told me he owed no child support to anyone, neither present nor past. In fact, he claimed, he didn't even have any children. I reworded the question a few times, but Terry's story stayed the same. I was about to decide against taking the case because of Terry's lack of candor towards me, but I gave him one last chance. I told him that if he wasn't truthful when we go to court, he could be fined and charged with perjury. Well, my warning apparently frightened the truth out of him and he changed the story. Terry owed tens of thousands of dollars in child support payments in more than one state! Now that he had given me the full disclosure I needed, we could move forward with business. How did I know the amounts owed for the children were large? The large size of the dollar symbol told me. If it wasn't much he owed, I might have seen a normal-sized dollar bill or a smaller dollar sign. In this case, the image was exaggerated, and it was all I needed to figure out that the amount owed was sizeable.

Although Terry was unnerved by my persistence, I never told him how I knew about his debts. He tried relentlessly to pry out of me how I knew his personal business, thinking maybe one of his friends tipped me off. No one told me anything—it was Terry who ratted himself out with the clear-cut information sitting right behind him.

Saved from an Explosion

Here's a visual warning image I once received that pertained to my life. Recently, I was scheduled to meet someone for dinner after work. Before driving toward the restaurant, I thought I'd stop first at the health food store to pick up some much-needed items. From the store, I would drive directly to the restaurant and meet my friend. The health food store was ten minutes from my office, so I was sure that stopping there wouldn't interfere with my dinner plans. I thought my idea was a great one, so I worked quickly to complete the day's work in less than the usual time. As I was getting ready to leave, I checked the time by glancing at the clock that hangs on the wall directly across from my desk. I noticed the time was precisely 3:50 PM. I thought if I left at that moment, I would be at the health food store on the dot at 4:00 PM. As I was getting up from my desk and reaching for my coat, I clairvoyantly saw the instantaneous image of my great-grandfather looking upset, with his right hand up, palm facing me as if directing me to stop. I abruptly stopped and thought to myself, "What's this all about? What could possibly happen to me on the way to the health food store?" The image happened again, but it was now larger and closer to me with the added symbol of an old fashioned red metal fireman's hat. Both visual images told me of imminent danger.

These images frightened me so much that I decided not to go to the store. I sat back down at my desk and worked for the balance of the afternoon. When I prepared again to leave my office an hour and a half later, I didn't receive warning images of any kind. The danger had passed. When I got into my car and turned on the radio, the local news came on with the top story—at precisely 4:00 PM that day was a major explosion and fire. It occurred at exactly the spot where I always parked my car before going to the health food store! The explosion was so strong it was heard and felt blocks away. Needless to say, I felt incredibly grateful for the unsolicited warning, confident that I had trusted the image I had received as valid and reliable, and relieved that I had properly acted on it.

Understanding the depths of clairvoyance and its development takes time and dedication, but it's worth the effort. Let's now move on to clairaudience, another widely experienced sixth sense.

Clairaudience: Clear Hearing

Our ordinary sense of hearing is, of course, through the ears. Sixth sense hearing, also known as clairaudience, takes our ordinary sense of hearing and elevates it to a higher spiritual level. There are two ways to experience clairaudient messages. The first can best be described as words received inside the head just above the ears, but outside the person's thinking process. The best way to express it is half-thought, half-spoken word, different in sequence than one's thought patterns. Just by the sound of it, you know it's coming from another dimension. The sound can be like a squeak, squeal, or like the rapid, high-pitched, and almost indistinct chatter of very young children. It can sound neither male nor female. At other times, clairaudient messages can sound like they are being

21

transmitted from a hollow cavity, like a bucket, or like someone talking rapidly through their nose. Your ability to hear clairaudiently may not come easily at first, but don't worry. Clairaudience takes much practice because the sixth sense message is transmitted to you at a very high frequency, which is at times inaudible. However, it's just as possible to hear clairaudient messages as clearly as you hear spoken ones. If you ever experienced what sounded like a voice shouting your name upon waking up or at the time of a crisis, you've experienced clairaudience.

In addition to hearing words, music can also be transmitted clairaudiently. For example, a melody with special meaning to you and a departed loved one could be transmitted to you to give you comfort.

The Lead Ear

In general, people are not clairaudient in both ears. Normally, one ear is the "lead" clairaudient ear through which the messages will normally enter. Usually, the ear on the stronger side of your body is the lead ear—if you are right handed, your right ear is the lead ear, et cetera. However, in addition to identifying your lead ear, you should begin to acquaint yourself with clairaudient messages that arrive just above your ear. As was described previously, they sound like half-thought, half-spoken words. The sound will seem to be coming from the middle of your head, but initiated from an outside source instead of you.

A word of advice—don't try too hard to hear clairaudiently. If you do, you might not hear anything at all. The more open you are to receiving clairaudient communication, the more distinct the sound will be. For clairaudience to happen, it takes time, trust, and patience.

To help receive clairaudient messages more clearly, every night before you go to bed, give thanks for all the spiritual love and guidance you have in your life. Next, ask for a simple auditory message to be transmitted to you upon waking. Ask that it be clear and slow enough so you can hear it. In only a few days, you should at least hear your name being called. At first, the sound of a voice may startle you and cause you to lose the connection. Don't worry. You will hear the voice again. As time goes on, you will no longer be so startled. The sixth sense messages will come forth often and in a very solid and deliberate flow.

Now that we've got a foundation in clairaudience, let's look at how common clairaudience is in our lives.

Clairaudience as a Life Saver

A close friend of mine, Jeanette, was having very serious health problems. No matter what she did to help herself, she just kept getting sicker. One morning while in a deep sleep, a voice shouted three words to her, "Jeannette, wake up." The voice sounded like a deep male voice coming from outside her head. It enunciated each syllable distinctly and had a caring, but urgent and serious tone. Jeannette did as she was told, and woke up. She sat bolt upright on her bed very startled, wondering where the voice had come from. Later that same day, Jeannette's condition worsened. By nightfall, Jeannette decided to go to the hospital emergency room. While being examined, Jeannette told the attending doctor, Dr. Pinney, about the voice that woke her earlier that day. Jeannette didn't know how to describe the voice, except to say, "If love were a sound, I heard the sound of pure love."

As she explained what happened, Jeannette looked directly into Dr. Pinney's eyes, not sure if she wanted approval or verification about her experience. As Dr. Pinney intently listened, he smiled warmly. His kind eyes told her exactly what he was thinking. Dr. Pinney told Jeannette to be grateful for the heavenly warning, claiming that if she had continued sleeping that day, it was very likely she would not have woken—she probably would have died in her sleep. Jeannette's time on earth was obviously not up, but she needed help from the higher realms to stay here. After a short but difficult health battle, Jeannette now has her illnesses under control. In addition, Jeannette takes great comfort in knowing she is not alone. There are many spiritual helpers who watch over all of us, all the time.

Bad Temper

Years ago, I had a legal consultation with a potential client named Gary, a polite and expensively dressed business man. As we dove into the facts of the case, the words "bad temper" kept ringing in my ears. The more I heard the words, the louder they got. Although Gary had a cool and calm demeanor, I took the clairaudient advice and declined the case. I later heard from my colleague, Bill, that Gary had become his client. Gary turned out to be a real problem—his apparent calm disposition had exploded into a display of anger after being told of his likely legal fate, and it happened right there in Bill's office.

Bouncing Balls

As I was concluding a legal consultation and about to have Rosa, a nervous client, sign the official forms, I asked for my fee so work could begin. Rosa presented me with her personal check as payment, even though I specifically told her to bring a money order.

My clairaudient sense gave me an earful! The sound of bouncing balls was deafening. With that knowledge, I immediately handed Rosa's check back to her and asked her to bring me a money order. I never saw her again.

An interesting characteristic to note about clairaudient communication is that no matter how loud it is, usually only those to whom it is directed can hear it. So although the sound of bouncing balls was very loud in the office, only I could hear it because it was spiritually directed to me.

Too Cold-Hearted

What happens when you don't act on your clairaudient messages? A few years back, Beth met a love interest, Walter. At the moment of the meeting, Beth vividly heard the words "too cold-hearted." Those words should have been warning enough to not begin any type of relationship with Walter, but Beth didn't heed the warning and the two continued to date. Even though both of them had some good times, Walter eventually proved the message totally correct. The relationship ended and Beth's unheeded warning remained accurate—Walter's cold-heartedness was the reason for the breakup.

All Will Be Fine

As humans, we have to experience the good and the bad in life. Spiritual messages may not always divert us from danger, but they may give us comfort in knowing there is light at the end of the tunnel when the suffering is over, as the following will illustrate.

About ten years ago, I was in a hurry to leave my office for a 2:30 PM court hearing across town. Since traffic was normally heavy on the interstate around this time, I felt especially hurried. I grabbed my handbag and held on tight to my client's huge file as I darted out of my second floor office. I ran as fast as I could down the steep staircase leading to the back patio and the parking lot. On my way out, the heel of my shoe caught on the top step of the patio. I lost my balance, and since my hands were full, there was nothing for me to grab to stop my rapid plummet toward the ground. As I was falling and heading face first toward the concrete patio, I saw in a split second an image of myself with my nose and other facial bones broken and blood oozing from numerous facial cuts. But just as I was to hit the concrete, I experienced what felt like two large arms securely holding my entire body and flipping me 180 degrees. My left elbow hit the ground first, followed by my torso and the back of my head. When my elbow hit the ground, I heard a loud "crack" and felt agonizing pain shooting down my arm. Within seconds of hitting the ground, I felt like my entire being was put into a cocoon of loving embrace. I could not feel or hear any type of internal or external stimuli. The pain had left me. All I heard was the sweetest and clearest voice. It said to me with incredible warmth, love, and compassion, "Don't worry, all will be fine. Your elbow is broken, but they won't even cast it!"

Once the voice was gone, the loving embrace was also gone. It was as if a switch turned my entire being back to the reality channel. I could feel the hard concrete against my head and back. I knew I must have had a concussion and at least one broken bone. The pain in my elbow was getting worse. I began to feel very cold as the ambulance pulled up with the piercing sound of its siren. After several hours spent in the hospital emergency room, the clairaudient voice was correct. When the doctors completed their x-rays and reviewed their findings, they said the elbow was indeed broken, but they could not cast it. They explained if they put a cast on the elbow, the mobility of the elbow would be lost. The doctors sent me home with a sling to wear for twelve weeks. I did have much pain and lots of inconvenience with the broken elbow, but all was fine in the end, just like the loving voice promised.

Claircognizance: Clear Knowing

Now that we have a solid foundation of two of the ways the higher senses send us information, let's move to an even more mystical way to receive higher sense guidance. Claircognizance, referred to as "clear knowing," is a gift that is well worth cultivating, and there are several ways to experience it.

Claircognizance makes itself known by a clear and unshakable knowledge about someone, something, or someplace about which you had no previous knowledge. Let's say you meet someone for the first time, and immediately you know something about that person, such as their marital status, line of work, or the color of their car. Such knowledge doesn't come from anything the person said or did. Your knowledge of the person has nothing to do with demeanor—you just *know* it.

In addition, claircognizance can also be experienced as creative inspiration. Many people who work in the fields of music, writing, painting, and design experience claircognizance on a daily basis. Their inspiration may come at unusual times and places. A writer could be inspired for a book plot while stuck in a traffic jam, or wake up in the middle of the night with a great twist to a screenplay he or she is writing.

What is interesting about creativity from claircognizance is when you review your creative work, you may not consciously remember some or most of the thoughts or ideas that came to you. You act as a vessel for the information to pour through. At times, when you review the inspired work, you may be just as surprised as someone else who is viewing your work for the first time. You may feel as if someone else did it because you may remember very little of its creation. You may also notice—whether the work is a piece of art or a manuscript—both need little, if any, fixing.

As with all sixth sense messages, claircognizance can give you a call to action; it can guide you to an excellent opportunity, warn you to refrain from action, or even inspire you. As you develop your claircognizant ability, you will receive more and more unsolicited factual information about people, places, and things.

Trust the claircognitive messages you receive, even the somewhat unbelievable ones, and accept them for what they are. Do not judge them or try to explain them away. By being nonjudgmental, your sixth sense abilities will not only soar, but prove to be useful in all you do.

The Gifted Artist

I am acquainted with a world-renowned portrait painter, Adam, who at times remains in his portrait studio for up to three days at a time painting a masterpiece. During that time, Adam paints day and night, foregoing eating, sleeping, and even bathroom breaks! Adam's focus is 100 percent on his painting. He claims he does not remember most of the time spent on creative endeavors, as if he were in some type of trance. When his inspiration is over, he is none the worse for it. While it sounds unbelievable, after three days Adam has no drop in blood sugar and he is not even tired. He is just a bit dirty and a little hungry. What Adam does feel is an unexplainable "high" and a feeling of not being grounded for about a day after he ends his painting episode. Although Adam has painted masterpieces for decades, he remains in awe over each work of art he creates. Adam has a very well developed claircognizant sense. He appreciates his gift and always claims his work is not his but "God given."

The following examples also illustrate how claircognizance works in everyday life.

A Great Investment

My colleague, Hillary, never owned real estate, but as she walked past a high-rise condominium, she knew she had to buy a unit in that particular building. Although friends criticized her for moving too quickly on such a major purchase, a well-developed claircognitive sense guided Hillary to purchase the condominium. To Hillary's delight, the condominium increased in value fivefold within ten months from the date she bought it. Hillary trusted her claircognizance and made a very wise decision.

Saving a Friend

Patsy got together with one of her childhood friends, Chas, for dinner. She hadn't seen him for almost a year, and as soon as they met, Patsy received a clear claircognitive message Chas was having very serious health problems, specifically diabetes and high blood pressure. Both conditions needed to be immediately addressed.

Patsy told Chas not to ask her any questions, just to listen to her. She told him to get a check-up because she was worried about him. The intense look in Patsy's eyes frightened Chas so much that he saw his doctor the next day. As it turned out, Patsy was right. Chas had out of control diabetes and high blood pressure, but because he received the proper medical care, he stopped what could have been complicated and life threatening conditions. He remains forever grateful for Patsy's insistence.

Malcolm Loves the Ladies

I recently met a blind musician named Malcolm. When we were introduced, I immediately received claircognitive information that he was a "ladies' man." My claircognizance told me Malcolm's list of conquests were as long as his arm. I accepted the information for what it was, even though it was absolutely contradictory to what he had told me about his life. Malcolm told me he missed his late wife so much, and he had become very depressed. He lived most days in solitude and didn't go out much. The information he shared with me was completely contradictory to what I received claircognitively. But, I still trusted the claircognitive information as accurate because of my experience and confidence working with it. Without any mention of my information, one of Malcolm's brothers said to me "don't believe anything that guy says. He's a real Casanova in this town." The moral of the story is—trust the claircognitive information you receive. It is accurate.

"Knowing" Another's Grief

Recently, I toured a historic mansion. As I walked to one corner of the first floor parlor, I was immediately aware of intense sadness—in fact, I became so overwhelmed by grief that I felt sick to my stomach, a bit faint, and had the overwhelming urge to cry. Then the facts unfolded and the story itself was transmitted claircognitively. Apparently, the woman of the house would sit in the corner crying because three of her little children had died. I also knew claircognitively the children died of sickness, and not from an external cause such as a fire or accident. Their mother's grief was unbelievable. When I entered the upstairs bedrooms, I saw pictures of six very young and beautiful children on display. As I approached the photos, I knew it was three of those children pictured who were the subject of the grief I experienced. Although there was much documentation about the family who inhabited the home, there was no mention of the cause of death of the three children, only their dates of birth and death below their portraits. Before I left, I spoke to the mansion's historian who verified the messages I received. The historian said that three of the six children died from influenza. Their mother would sit downstairs in the parlor for hours crying and remaining self-absorbed in her unspeakable loss. The mother died a few years after her children. Although many years passed between the time of her losses and my visit, the house itself was full of information that made its way to me through claircognizance.

By this point, you should feel very enthused about all the information that is available and ready to make its way to you simply for the asking.

Clairsentience: Clear Feeling

Clairsentience, known as "clear feeling," is also known as the "gut feeling" or one's intuition. Some authors consider the intuition as part of claircognizance, but I do not. I consider intuition as being related to clairsentience because of the feeling we get in our *gut*—it's less to do with the brain, and more to do with the center of the body.

Clairsentience is the most mainstream or widely accepted form of sixth sense communication. It is experienced by many for the big and little decisions in life, as well as the split-second decisions resulting in life-changing events.

The information received through the intuition comes from the spiritual realm and is relayed to you for your highest good. Because of the intuition's heavenly origins, it should come as no surprise to you that when people follow their intuition or gut feeling, the outcome is usually favorable. Why do people go against their intuition and make a decision contrary to it, especially in the area of choosing a romantic partner? Because the information they receive is not congruous to what suits them. When anyone takes intuitive information and rejects or reasons it to the contrary, they've gone against spiritual information. When you go against spiritual information, you repent in leisure for the mistake itself and all its life-affecting negative repercussions and long-term damaging effects.

Normally, you cannot go more than a day without hearing someone on television or radio relay a story that has something to do with intuition. Many such stories have to do with emergency personnel, such as a police officer who did a car check on a "hunch" that the driver was in some way wanted by the authorities, resulting in the arrest of a "most wanted" fugitive; or we may hear of a kidnapping that was solved due to a police officer acting on a hunch or feeling that "something just didn't seem right" about a child who was with a strangely behaving adult. You don't need to experience intuition so dramatically or on a superhero level—you can experience intuition all day and every day for the small things in life too!

Where do you feel the hunch of the intuition? You get the hunch (sometimes called the nudge) in the gut, also known as the solar plexus, our body's largest energy center. The majority of sensory phenomena that enter and leave the body and its surrounding energy field do so through the solar plexus. The solar plexus is considered the major conduit from the vast universal consciousness to the mind, body, and spirit.

The solar plexus's condition is crucial to the proper functioning of clairsentience and the proper energy functioning of the body. The solar plexus is a very good holistic indicator of one's overall strength and vitality. When the body is at peak performance, the solar plexus is also normally looking its best. The muscles and skin at the site of the solar plexus speak to its condition. If they are smooth and firm, not hard or loose to the touch, the solar plexus is doing well.

When your solar plexus is not functioning well, you experience physical, emotional, and spiritual problems. Physically, the solar plexus area on the body will feel tender, slightly warmer, and maybe even dry and scaly. You may have difficulty standing up straight and breathing deeply. Digestion and food absorption will be deficient. Emotionally, you may experience any number of extreme feelings—real or imagined. Spiritually, you may experience confusion and disordered thinking about your importance and your purpose in life. Think back to a time when you had physical, emotional, or spiritual sickness. No doubt, your solar plexus was not in optimal condition. It is interesting to note that the solar plexus of people who are grieving a major life loss is always weak, irregular in shape, and slow in energetic flow. The next time you are at a funeral, watch for what I call the solar plexus rub. Mourners normally rub the area just below the rib cage as an instinctive action to help stimulate or strengthen the body's weak solar plexus. The body instinctively knows if the solar plexus becomes stronger, the body, mind, and spirit will be stronger.

In addition to those experiencing grief, the solar plexus is tender to the touch on people who worry excessively, or who are constantly tired due to their demanding lives. Chronic worry and tiredness and the resulting negative effect on the solar plexus are not good for one's overall vitality, long-term health, and sixth sense development. Once a person's physical and emotional energies are replenished, the solar plexus becomes strong again and the intuition is up and running at full potential.

Intuition is a natural and important skill to develop. Please devote even a few seconds a day to exercising your intuition. It's simple to do. Begin by mentally relaxing and focusing on the area around your gut or solar plexus where the intuitive "nudge" is felt. When your mind is clear, ask yourself a question with a yes or no answer, such as, "Will I get the job I just interviewed for?" Immediately pay attention to how you feel in the gut. Do you feel a momentary good, calm feeling coming from the solar plexus? If so, the outcome should be positive. If you feel a momentary sick or sinking feeling, your answer is most likely negative. Get accustomed to subtle differences in feeling. Do this exercise every day, keeping notes of your gut feeling and the resulting outcome. The more the feeling and the outcome match, the more advanced your intuition has become.

As you develop your clairsentience, you become more sensitive to the natural world. You will sense and differentiate the unique feelings and energies of different animals. If you visit a zoo, after experiencing the awe of seeing in person the many beautiful animals from all over the world, your clairsentience may kick in and you may sense their unnatural life style and their frustration of not being able to live free. You may eventually be able to feel the energies of things we consider nonliving, such as a large rock formation; perhaps you may feel the many centuries of pressure it underwent to get to where it is today. You may also begin to clairsentiently feel the strong vitality, solidness, and strength of large trees on the one end of the continuum and the delicateness of a little flower on the other.

Many wonder if clairsentience and empathy are the same. By definition, there's a fine line of difference between them, but in practice, they can overlap. Clairsentience is awareness of, or describing of, an energy vibration a person feels. Even though you may actually physically and/or emotionally feel what another is feeling (such as their pain, sadness, or discomfort), you are not absorbing or aligning with it. It's still what I consider an external perception. Empathy, on the other hand, is defined as internalizing the feelings of others and really putting yourself in their shoes. Although I view them differently, you can still experience both at the same time.

Besides the gut feeling response and the increased sensitivity you have to your surroundings, clairsentience is also present when you intuitively feel your body's reaction to something present but physically invisible. I'm sure this has happened to you at least once in your life—you walk into a room and feel very uplifted for no apparent reason. What you experienced was actually a very spiritual phenomenon known as clairsentience. Your gut or solar plexus was able to read a strong positive energy that remained in the room long after the occupants left. Let's now look at the opposite. If you walk into a room and feel agitation or sadness, or if the atmosphere feels so heavy you can cut it with a knife, you are again experiencing clairsentience. An argument may have happened just before you walked into the room and that energy has remained.

Practically speaking, what good is it to have well-developed clairsentient ability? There's so much good to be had for listening to the gut feeling and acting on this spiritual information, even for the everyday things in life. Let's assume you are thinking of renting an apartment or buying a home—if you focus on your gut you should be able to determine if the apartment or house "feels right" or wrong. It is always better live in a place where you have a good gut feeling because it will more likely be a place of peace, contentment, and beneficial personal growth. In addition, if you have well-developed clairsentience, your gut feeling will be a great additional help in making proper decisions about what you need in life for your spiritual journey. When you listen to your gut, you will make fewer mistakes. Synchronicity will enter your life and become commonplace. Your sensitivity to all that's around you will increase, making you more aware of opportunities in life, and warning you about danger.

Let's now step away from the textual explanation and look at the way clairsentience or intuition makes itself known in your life in ordinary ways

Money Saved from Listening to the Gut

As said before, intuition is helpful for the big, as well as the smaller, more routine things in life. Sometimes, however, the so-called smaller decisions can become major problems of inconvenience and wasted money if not properly addressed.

I recently needed replacement windows installed in my house, and I was ready to hire a particular contractor. I called and asked him to stop in for the estimate. When we met and he shook my hand, I received the clear intuitive gut feeling to not hire him. I didn't know what the reason behind the feeling was, but I listened to my intuition. That decision proved later to be correct. Several months after my window estimate, he was the subject of one of the top news stories in the region. The man was arrested on numerous charges of taking money up front from consumers for whom he never purchased windows or returned to install. By going with my gut, I saved thousands of dollars, and lots of time and aggravation.

What Does Intuition Have to Do with Pet Adoption?

On a lighter note, my intuition helped me years ago to choose a pet (a cat) who proved to be a great companion, even though someone at the adoption center advised me against adopting him.

I was told this particular cat had been at the center for almost a year and was not friendly, so would not make a good pet. But when I looked into the cat's eyes, my intuition told me to give him a chance. He had probably been confined to a cage too long and needed to get out and be part of someone's family. Once he had time to adjust, his friendly disposition would shine. I decided to go against what I was told because my strong intuition told me otherwise.

I took him home. My intuition was correct. DJ turned out to be the friendliest and most fun pet I ever had. To this day, I am thankful—for his sake and mine—that I relied on my own sixth sense and not someone else's opinion.

At this point, we have a good, solid foundation of understanding the sixth sense. There are three more "clairs" I'd like to discuss, but in not as much detail as the others.

Clairtangency: Clear Touch

Some label clairtangency or "clear touch" under claircognizance because of the automatic knowledge it delivers. Others claim clairtangency belongs to clairsentience for the feelings one can experience when it happens. I like to discuss it separately for its own identity and benefits. Let's begin with a well-known practice commonly referred to as psychometry. Psychometry allows you to receive psychic information from touch alone. Years ago, there were many television demonstrations of psychometry where a psychic would handle an object and give the audience unsolicited information about the person who owned it. You can do this too. It's very easy—hold anything that belongs to someone else. Close your eyes, and while holding it, allow your sixth sense feelings and knowledge to kick in.

Clairtangency is also widely used by some medical intuitives who use touch on their patients to determine the existence of diseased energy. Among many methods—from feeling hot spots or cold spots to feeling a disorganized energy flow in and around the body or particular organs—the medical intuitive can use clairtangency in addition to other methods to diagnose and treat disease.

Clairtangency can also be experienced as the feeling of physical contact with a departed loved one. This contact can be either in a dream or in a deep meditative state and can be experienced, for example, as the touch of the hand of a departed loved one. Some claim to sense their guardian angel nearby watching over them and giving them protection. Some have claimed to feel the unexplainable loving clairtangent touch of an angel, as in the following example.

Laura's Angel

Upon waking from time to time, Laura would see an angel's huge wing near her right arm, and occasionally would feel it brush against her with an indescribable softness. Although the feeling was an indescribably beautiful sixth sense experience, it was always the signal of an approaching tragedy. Laura viewed the clairtangent gift as a way to mentally prepare herself for difficulties soon to come. She also believed the angel was giving her spiritual strength and telling her to not feel alone, reaffirming its closeness and readiness to offer comfort and support.

Clairolfaction: Clear Scent

Clairolfaction is the ability to perceive scents through the psychic senses. It usually happens when a person is watching television or reading a book, for example, and suddenly smells his or her departed mother's perfume or an uncle's favorite cologne. Some people who visit the shrines of saints claim to smell the most unbelievably heavenly fragrance similar to the most sweet-smelling perfume imaginable. The experience is believed to be a true gift and blessing because it is said to be a direct contact between the saint and the person. Many have experienced a psychic scent as very fragrant, heavy, and strong. At times, it almost takes the person's breath away. It's interesting to note that a person sitting next to the clairolfactant may not necessarily smell the same thing at all.

How does one develop clairolfaction? I have always viewed this gift as an outgrowth of overall psychic development, similar to being proficient at learning Spanish, and therefore, having an easy time picking up Italian. If your psychic abilities have been developed, and are therefore more elevated, when you need the sense of smell to more fully understand a message or to experience a spiritual connection, it will come forth on its own.

Grandpop's Tobacco

Paul's grandfather loved smoking his pipe. He loved it so much that all the grandchildren would joke that he and the pipe were inseparable. Grandpop could always be seen puffing away at his favorite tobacco, which was the one with the distinct blueberry scent. The tobacco smell was so strong that it made everyone cough and sneeze.

Due to a career move from his hometown in upstate Pennsylvania to Denver, Paul reluctantly moved away. He missed his Grandpop terribly. One night when Paul was working late on financial statements at his computer, the smell of Grandpop's blueberry tobacco overcame him. At that same moment, Paul burst into tears. With uncontrollable sobs, Paul knew his beloved Grandpop had died. Although broken-hearted, Paul will never forget the momentary connection he had at the moment of his Grandpop's death. Paul says that in that moment, he had the strongest, most powerful, and loving feeling he had ever felt for his Grandpop. The incident gives Paul a feeling of comfort when he pines for his Grandpop's companionship.

Clairgustance: Clear Taste

Overall, clairgustance is not as widely experienced as the other senses. It is what I call a supplementary sixth sense, or a sixth sense for a limited purpose. Your favorite aunt may have passed years ago, but when she was alive, made the best cheesecake imaginable. Lately, you find yourself missing her. Upon rising from a nap, you may taste her famous cheesecake for a split second. You don't actually have a slice of cheese cake in your mouth—you just have a fleeting moment of spiritual taste!

Just like clairtangency, this ability is used by some medical intuitives who have the distinct ability to "taste" disease. The taste simply happens and is very useful and helpful to the clairgustant's holistic medical practice. From the foul spiritual taste of cancer to the spiritual taste of diabetes' cloying sweetness, some medical intuitives are able to add to their solid knowledge base—their sixth sense—to treat their patients.

Lorraine's Tasty Connection

In the days before Lorraine died, she continuously claimed to taste every one of her mother's tasty German dishes. At or near mealtimes, the distinct taste of a different favorite food came to her. Lorraine would close her eyes and enumerate all the flavors of those homemade dishes prepared so many years ago, none of which were there. After each such episode, Lorraine appeared to be satisfied and full, even though she ate nothing in the days before her death.

Lorraine was lucid to the end, and she believed the remembrances of past meals, especially the tasty treats of holidays past, must have been her mom's way of saying, "We're waiting for you to come home and experience all those things again." Well, come home she did, peacefully and with a beautiful smile on her face as she passed.

PART II

The A–Z Guide

Now that we have an excellent foundation in sixth sense concepts and how valuable they are to your life, let's move on to the A–Z guide, a twenty-six-letter mnemonic method I believe will help make recall of the tools in this book easy and fun to experience. Years after reading this book, you will instantly remember chapter contents just by thinking of their corresponding letter. Although the book is set up to help you recollect the principles easily, I suggest you keep it as a reference manual for your lifelong journey of sixth sense development. Refer to it often by reading and re-reading it in your spare time to help you keep these spiritual principles active in your life. Spend time thinking about the examples and stories contained in each chapter. Think about your own similar experiences and the effect those experiences had

59

on your own life. As you read and re-read the chapters, add your own thoughts, feelings, and opinions. Expand the material and make it a real working document.

Remember, there is nothing suspect or mysterious about heightening the senses—it is one of the most natural things to do. Just as you can have a better toned body by exercising and eating right, or achieve better test scores by studying more, so too can you have a more magical life by heightening your sixth sense.

Awareness

The first tool to develop the sixth sense begins with the letter A and it is the most appropriate first step in developing your higher senses as well. "A" is for awareness.

Awareness is all about deep perception and insight. Awareness means training yourself to be more observant of your surroundings. By focusing on awareness, you train yourself to become more open to all the sensory information around you.

Although the act of being aware may sound almost elementary, it's an important lesson for us to learn, especially today when we often spend the majority of our days in the same routine, and tuning things *out*. We routinely go to work at the same time and by the same travel route. We perform our jobs according to the same well-defined procedures, return home at the same time, eat the same types of foods, and do the same housework. We often watch the same television shows, go to bed at about the same time, and we rise in the morning at the same time by the sound of the same alarm clock. The list of routine goes on and on. Of course, predictability has its positive aspects, but it can also lead to a bit of stagnation, counteracting the development of our higher senses.

Consider the blockbuster movie, *The Sixth Sense*, written and directed by M. Night Shyamalan. This movie is probably the best proof of widespread sensory unawareness. Shyamalan used his genius and a common societal fault of sensory unawareness to bring a twist to this blockbuster movie. The movie opens with psychologist Dr. Malcolm Crowe, played by actor Bruce Willis, returning home after receiving an award from the city of Philadelphia for his dedication and excellence in the field of child psychology. He is confronted in his bedroom by one of his former patients, Vincent Grey, who shoots Dr. Crowe and turns the gun on himself. The movie then shows what appears to be a recovered Dr. Crowe who meets and works with Cole Sear, a shy nine-year-old boy who has been experiencing visions of the dead. He lives in a constant state of fear and anxiety and doesn't understand what is happening around him. Cole is withdrawn, and his schoolwork and relationships have suffered. As Dr. Crowe spends more time with Cole, he realizes Cole's symptoms are like that of Vincent's. After careful analysis, Dr. Crowe shifts his focus away from Cole as having a problem, to the dead and what they may want from him. Together, Dr. Crow and Cole discover that the dead are coming to Cole for help because he can see them with his sixth sense. With that change in perception, Cole loses the fear, becoming happier, more extroverted, and better adjusted. Cole is now accepted by his peers. The focus then turns to Dr. Crowe who examines his marriage. A scene turns to Dr. Crowe's wife, Anna, who is lying in bed. As she tosses a wedding band on the floor, she half-asks, half declares, "Malcolm, why did you leave me?" We then see her own wedding band on her finger, causing Dr. Crowe to realize that he never survived the shooting. Not only is Dr. Crowe shocked that he's been dead all along, but the audience is too. Why? The clues that Dr. Crowe died at the beginning of the movie were in every scene. His clothes were never different than the ones he wore and touched on the day he died. There was no rapport or interaction between him and anyone else in the movie except for Cole. However, even with the many hints and clues, very few viewers realized Dr. Crowe was dead. What set most people up for the big twist at the end? Their own sensory unawareness!

Exercises to Improve Awareness

To counteract sensory unawareness, you can simply pay keen attention to your everyday life. It may seem overwhelming at first, but after a little while, it becomes second-nature. Try the following two exercises, which can be done one after the other. They each take less than a minute to do.

First, when you sit down to your next meal, really look at the food in your plate. Do the colors of the food look appetizing or dull? Smell the food. Does the food smell so mouth-watering you cannot wait to dig in? Take a bite. Savor each and every flavor. Notice the combination of tastes. Is what you taste sweet? Sour? Are any two combinations of flavors better than any two others? Which flavor is your favorite? Do this exercise consciously until it becomes habit.

The second exercise works best if done in the outdoors. Hold a small flower in your hand. I prefer a flower for its effect on multiple senses, but if you are unable to find a flower, even a blade of grass or a small object, such as a glass figurine will work. The main emphasis is the object must be small enough to hold in your hands. Let's assume you picked a flower from your garden, and you are now holding it. What is the first thing that comes to your mind about this flower: its fragrance, color, or even its softness against your hand? Take a moment to look closely at a minute detail of the flower, for example, a small spot of color on one of the petals. While still holding the flower, stretch your arm as far from your body as you can to look at the flower as a whole. Do a quick scan of all your senses. For example, what do you see, smell, and feel about this flower? If you could "hear" this flower, what would it sound like? Imagine if you were to taste the flower, what would it taste like? Simply be aware of the flower on all sensory levels.

Do the second awareness exercise for one week, varying your subject matter each day. Once you have spent a week doing the two exercises listed here, extend your awareness to the feelings you get when you are around people and places. Let's begin with a short exercise focusing on the affect positive people have on you. I want you now to be especially aware of how you feel when you think about someone you really love or with whom you like to spend lots of time. We will refer to this special person as your SP. Your SP can be anyone—a parent, spouse, partner, or a very close friend. Whoever it is, be aware of the physical, emotional, and spiritual changes you feel at the moment you are in the SP's presence. When you are with your SP, does your heart beat differently than when you are with other people? When you're with your SP, do you feel safe and secure on all levels? Do you have a feeling of inner strength, or do you simply feel very content and at peace? Do you smile and laugh more in your SP's presence? Do you feel more complete as a person when you are with him or her? In addition, what is it about your SP that's different from everyone else with whom you have contact? What is the spiritual bond that ties you to each other? If your SP has passed, you can still do this exercise. Rely on your memory to reflect on the positive physical, emotional, and spiritual effects this person has had on you.

Next, I want you to experience the opposite. Be aware of how you feel when you interact with negative people. When you are with negative people, how do you feel physically, emotionally, and spiritually? Do you feel dragged down, sleepy, or maybe even agitated and nasty? Now switch your focus to one specific negative person. Are you aware of a feeling of heaviness or darkness around him or her? Begin cultivating an awareness of the physical, emotional, and spiritual differences you feel when near positive people opposed to how you feel around negative people.

Once you have become very adept at being aware, take your awareness to a higher level when you are around new people, places, and situations. For example, when you are walking along a street you've never been on before, focus on a particular house on that street, of which you know nothing. Become aware of how you feel as you approach and pass by the house. Do you feel an element of mystery or maybe an unexplained feeling of happiness? Do you feel love or maybe coldness?

As an additional method of taking awareness to a higher level, whenever you are introduced to someone, do what I call an *instant awareness scan*. When you first meet someone, look instantaneously into his or her eyes and, if possible, make physical contact through a handshake. In a split second, be aware of the first thing that comes to mind about this person. Be open and do not dismiss what comes through. Sometimes what comes through to you may not match the person's friendly smile or appearance. Keep in mind—you will meet many masters of camouflage along the way. Just keep taking your awareness to a higher level and your sixth sense benefits will unfold.

Breathing

I believe there can be no true sixth sense development without deep, calm, purposeful breathing. Along with awareness, I view purposeful breathing as the foundation to advanced sixth sense development.

Purposeful breathing is just that—the use of breathing as a higher sense development tool. Purposeful, focused, diaphragmic breathing will help you open your intuition and any higher sense of your choosing. Because it is focused, purposeful breathing is a much slower, deeper, and more rhythmic breathing than the usual more shallow breathing most people do.

You should train yourself to breathe deeply all the time for its good health benefits, but I want you to focus on your purposeful breathing as a sixth sense tool to move your awareness to a higher level. I recommend you practice your breathing as much as you can—the more you do it, the better and longer you will sustain it and the more sixth sense benefits you will reap.

Step-by-Step Purposeful Breathing

Begin by choosing a specific location in your residence you will now consider your sacred space or place. This is where you will do your purposeful breathing. Your sacred space can be as small or as large as you want, but it should be clean, quiet, orderly, and peaceful. I suggest that you don't play any music, not even ambient or classical. While this music does promote calmness, different musical notes stimulate different energy centers in the body, which may interfere with this exercise. The benefits of music as a sixth sense tool are discussed later in this book. For now, just keep the sacred space quiet.

Now that you've chosen your sacred space, you'll need a chair or a floor mat. Whatever you choose, make sure it is made of a natural material. When you make physical contact with natural material, the natural material itself acts as a conduit of energy by its innate ability. Please do not do your purposeful breathing in an overstuffed chair, couch, or in bed, otherwise you may fall asleep.

Sit upright in the chair or on the floor, chin parallel to the floor. Clear your head of internal chatter. When your head is clear, begin to inhale through the nose slowly, deeply, and purposefully. Next, slowly exhale through the mouth. Focus on every aspect of inhaling and exhaling along with its mind and body effects. Do you feel the body relax? What is it about your body that feels so calm? Be aware of your body's changes as you reach a state of relaxation. Do you feel changes in your entire body—from your head to your feet—as you inhale and exhale? Do you feel your stress and tension dissipating? You should begin to feel a type of full-body relaxation that is indescribable. You may even hear vertebra in your neck or in your back click into place. Along with the feeling of relaxation, you should begin to feel a somewhat energized state of heightened awareness.

If you feel all of this, you have properly used breathing as a tool for sixth sense development and are ready to move forward to the next stage. If you have not yet reached an energized state of awareness, just keep practicing. You will reach it, but do not move onto the next stage until you do.

While remaining upright in the chair or on the floor with your eyes closed, take one hand and place it on top of the other on the solar plexus, which is located just below the rib cage. Continue the purposeful breathing as the body continues to relax and expand its awareness. Now, direct your awareness to the top of your head. Imagine it has opened wide to let in the positive and all-encompassing universal energy. Maintain the focus for as long as you can, but no less than a minute. You may now feel slightly light-headed and notice a change in the energy in and around the cheeks, on your forehead, and your crown.

Next, move your focus from the top of your head to your solar plexus, where your hands remain folded, one on the other. Focus on your solar plexus and envision it as open to the positive and all-encompassing, vast, universal energy. Once you move your focus to the solar plexus, you may feel a slight burst of energy in and around that region. If you do, great! You are becoming sensitive to changes in internal and external energy. If you don't feel anything, that's okay too. You just need a little more time for your energy sensitivity to become a bit more refined and developed. Take heart in knowing that whether or not you feel these changes, the energy is still moving rapidly. Your sixth sense development is advancing by leaps and bounds.

That is all there is to purposeful breathing. Although it seems simple and easy, the sixth sense affects are profound. Remember, especially at the beginning of your practice, you will likely lose your focus and concentration. Just return your attention to the action of inhaling and exhaling and your focus will return.

Besides its benefits to heightening the senses, deep purposeful breathing has its own natural health-promoting benefits. No matter when you do it, deep purposeful breathing helps to generally make you more alert and feel more rested. Deep breathing also opens the throat and allows your voice to sound more relaxed, strong, and rhythmic in tone. Deep purposeful breathing helps your mind to be more centered. You will be more productive and spend less time on menial tasks. The benefits alone from proper deep breathing for your job, schoolwork, and your life in general are profound.

Practice the breathing exercise for as long or as short a time as you like. Some sixth sense practitioners believe deep breathing done often is all you need to open the psychic channels; therefore, if you focus solely on purposeful breathing with no other changes to your sixth sense regime, your sixth sense should automatically develop quickly on its own.

Colors

Color is a fascinating reflection of our internal and external energy. The color of our energy field tells the world who we are. We normally incorporate the color of our energy field in everything related to us without consciously realizing it. Let's begin with a discussion of the mechanics and colors of the chakra system. We'll then move on to an exercise to heighten your chakra awareness, and then look at the affect the colors in our energy field, including the chakras, have on our choices of food, clothing, and surroundings.

Chakras

The human body is composed not only of bones, flesh, and blood, but also of a whole other intricate, energy system that makes us who we are. The chakra system, composed of seven major energy centers and hundreds of minor ones, creates an unseen, interlocking, and constantly changing energy structure on, in, and around the body. Each chakra is connected to a different body part or organ. What occurs in each of the seven chakras affects the body part or organ to which it is attached and vice versa.

The shapes, colors, and movement of each of the energy centers are like that of the spokes of a brightly colored wheel, continuously processing all the energy that flows into and out of us. Just merely thinking of the energetic complexity of the chakra system can fill us with gratitude and awe for our existence.

Everyone has the same number of chakras, and each chakra has the same importance to one's well-being, but the condition of each chakra and chakra system is as individual as fingerprints. Each chakra differs from everyone else's in size, shade of color, and shape. In addition, the energy flow through the chakras differs from person to person in its direction, rhythm, pattern, intensity, and speed. On one person, for example, the third chakra may be larger and more vibrant, while on another that same chakra may be substantially smaller.

As your senses become more and more heightened, you will be able to energetically perceive the chakras. Once you tune in to the chakra system with your heightened senses, not only will you spiritually see the energy flow—you will also feel, know, and hear the intense vigorous swirling energy of each of the chakras through your heightened senses.

Following is a description of each of the major chakras—their location, function, and color when at peak performance. This book's discussions will focus mostly on the third, sixth, and seventh chakras.

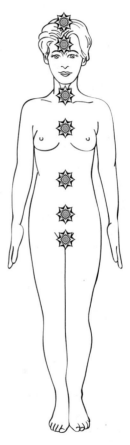

The Major Chakra System

Name	Where Located	Function	Healthy Color
1. Root	Base of the spine	Self Preservation	Red
2. Sacral	Over the spleen	Basic Emotional Needs	Orange
3. Solar Plexus	Just above the navel	Willpower and Intuition	Yellow
4. Heart	Center of the chest	Higher Consciousness/ Universal Love	Green
5. Throat	Between the neck and larynx	Creativity and Self Expression	Blue
6. Third Eye	Between the eyebrows	Heightened Sense of Sight	Indigo
7. Crown	Top of the head	Highest Level of Consciousness	Violet

Healthy Chakras

An open chakra is a healthy chakra that evidences one's physical, emotional, and spiritual health are at peak performance. A healthy chakra looks like a four- or five-inch wheel of clear, bright, vibrant, and beautiful colors swirling rhythmically with a shimmering effect, like the sheen of an opal or mother-of-pearl. The collective sound of healthy chakras on the body is like the calming purr of a cat, or the soft hum of a well-functioning motor. How fast the energy is moving, as well as its sound, weight, and rhythm, all relate to the physical, emotional, and spiritual health of the person.

For those readers who are animal lovers, animals also have a chakra system. In fact, the chakras of animals are beautiful displays of bright light and color vibrancy. Domesticated pets have huge heart chakras. Animals in the wild have stronger root chakras.

Cleansing the Chakra System

Although you will soon become an expert at evaluating the chakras of others, you must also maintain your own healthy chakra system so your sixth sense abilities are able to advance.

To keep the chakras healthy, open, and working at optimal performance, it's helpful to do a daily spiritual cleanse of the chakra system, a process that takes only a few minutes. Begin with deep breathing. As you breathe deeply with your eyes closed, focus first on the top of your head at the seventh (crown) chakra. Next, visualize a beam of white healing light coming from the heavens and entering through the top of your head, stopping momentarily at every chakra. When the light has entered the last chakra, allow it to disperse with love and gratitude, ending the session.

The clear healing light acts as a cleansing rod of energy, removing all negativity, including stickiness or heaviness, from each and every chakra. This exercise is a great spiritual, mental, and physical clearing exercise. It is also a great exercise to improve your thinking process, your judgment, and your general awareness.

Weak Chakras

When a chakra is not functioning at its best due to physical, emotional, or spiritual troubles, it will become smaller and more irregular in shape. It will measure about one or two inches in diameter, less than half of the size of a healthy one. A weak chakra is open just enough to allow in the minimal divine life force. As a chakra becomes smaller, its energy becomes stagnant. It has difficulty flowing freely, and the organ to which it is connected becomes more and more inactive. The energy rhythm of the chakra becomes chaotic.

No one can be at peak performance with one or more constricted chakras. In addition to the restricted and chaotic energy flow, when a chakra is not functioning at its best, its colors are dull and muddy.

At the end of our lives, when the body experiences a natural death, the chakra system gradually shrinks and closes up. The chakras are gone when we die.

Practice Heightened Senses with Chakra Observation

The best place to practice applying your sixth sense knowledge of chakras is in a health care setting. If you work in a hospital, nursing home, doctor's office, or any other health care facility, you have all the subjects you need to observe and assess chakra energy. First, choose a particular chakra that you wish to observe, and then compare and contrast the differences of that chakra in everyone you meet. By "specializing" in one chakra at a time, you begin to amass a continuum of similarities and differences. In other words, you will soon become a chakra energy expert. To illustrate how this works, assume you choose the throat chakra as the one you wish to study. You may observe the throat chakras of throat cancer patients, comparing and contrasting their energy to each other and distinguishing their energy flow from the throat chakras of healthy people. Notice the difference in size, color, vibrancy, and energy flow. Continuously refine your power of awareness to focus and differentiate between healthy and unhealthy chakras and chakra systems. Observe age groups. What are the differences, both obvious and subtle, between chakras of the very young and old? You will quickly become a chakra expert and without effort, increase your sensitivity to energy while developing your sixth sense abilities.

The Crown Chakra

I would like to direct your attention for a moment to the seventh chakra, the crown chakra. When a person is truly committed to a selfless life's work or has an attitude of sincere selfless love, the strength and direction of the seventh chakra's energy is that of an outward radiation. In other words, beautiful, loving, and rhythmic energy flows not only into the person, but more strongly flows out of the person to all of humanity. If your sixth sense is really developed, you will notice or sense the outward energy flow on a person with a strong crown chakra as a heavy concentration of energy at the top of the head. In religious paintings, this type of energy is depicted as a halo above the heads of saints. A strong display of energy from the seventh chakra is not commonplace. You may only experience a very developed crown chakra a few times in your life. When you do, you will feel a sense of honor to be in the presence of such a special person. As an aside, if you ever meet someone with such a strong crown chakra, take notice of the affect they have on your energy. You will feel a magnetism drawing you to them in a positive, uplifting way. Their positive energetic affect on you will last from a few hours to a few days after leaving their presence. If their energy is really strong, it can have a profound life altering affect on you, and may even trigger instantaneous positive, lifelong changes for you. Many people who met Mother Teresa, even for a few minutes, felt this way. They claimed their lives were changed forever.

Colors and Food

Few colors affect us more intimately than the colors of the foods we consume. Consuming beautiful colors helps heal and energize the chakras. To illustrate this concept, look at the colors of the typical fast food plate. They are dull and drab, a "sea of beige," consisting of French fries, buns, and onion rings. Now look at the bright, vibrant colors of a plate of fresh vegetables. If you eat a diet rich in the vivid colors of natural foods, you will feel and look like the energy of the food: bright, beautiful, and healthy. The beauty of the food and its nutrients will help make your energy more positive. Along with feeling better physically, you will also feel calmer and more at peace. You don't need to make these choices complicated, however.

Simply choose food that makes the plate look like a beautiful color palette.

You may be wondering, what do the colors of your food have to do with sixth sense development? When you nourish the energy inside your body, you also improve your internal energy, including the chakra system. Your physical, emotional, and spiritual systems will function better, which will in turn facilitate sixth sense development.

Colors and Clothes

Along with the color of the foods we eat, it's important to look at the color of your clothing. The colors you choose to wear project the state of your health; your inner thoughts, feelings, moods; and the condition of your chakras. In addition, clothing color also acts as an energy attractor and repellent.

When you choose your clothing, really think about the colors, their relationship to the energy you wish to project and attract, and the chakras you wish to improve. If you wear dark, muddy colors, you project and attract negativity, which creates and attracts stagnation and more negativity. Negativity does not create newness or abundance on any level, such as new friendships, love, more money, better health, new career options, or more assets in general. To help counteract the attraction of negativity, try to wear or at least add bright clear colors to your wardrobe, preferably with the chakra chart in mind. By wearing such bright colors, you will project a more positive image and in return attract more positive energy, automatically repelling the negative. Women who wish to marry are often advised to wear red to attract a mate—and many have great results!

Let's try an easy experiment. Purposely wear drab clothes for a day. At the end of the day, analyze how you felt that day on every level. Were you energized? Did you feel confident? Did you have a positive outlook? Did you attract positive or negative experiences? The next day, do the completely opposite. Wear bright colors. At the end of the day, do the same analysis. You should experience a difference between the two days. The "happier" colors do more than make you look good—they work on chakra energy without you consciously knowing it. By improving chakra energy, you improve your overall energy vibration. With a positive magnetism, you open the door to positive experiences.

When I was in mourning over the loss of my father, I purposely chose clothing colors that were uplifting. The colors of my business suits were, for example, canary yellow, baby blue, and mint green. I noticed that by choosing colors of clothing that were bright and cheery, I had more periods of time when I felt more at peace, which helped me to stop thinking of my loss.

Colors and Surroundings

The colors you choose to display around your home have the same effect on your physical, spiritual, and emotional health. Your home is an extension of who you are. Look around your home, observe the colors of the ceilings, floors, furniture, walls, and wall décor. Do the colors blend and make you feel uplifted and contented? Are the colors drab, harsh, or in conflict with each other? Walk into each room of your house and think about how you feel. Do you feel relaxed and at peace? Do you feel happy? If not, begin by making small color changes to your surroundings. Maybe paint one wall or add a home accessory such as a vase or a small painting with colors that make you feel uplifted, calm, and peaceful. By continuing to add the right colors to your surroundings, you will not only feel better and begin to attract what is good and wholesome into your life, you will also help facilitate your sixth sense advancement.

Start today to focus on the colors in your life. Make changes! Add brightness and beauty! Your life and sixth sense development will benefit.

Dreaming

Dreams, those timeless sources of mystery and intrigue, are powerful sources of information. They provide inspiration for artists and writers, prophecies about events both large and small, and answers to life's most nagging problems and questions. Many people have advanced their sixth sense so much through their dreams that they rely almost totally on dreams to provide clues and answers to their problems, and inspiration for their work. People who have mastered the power of dreams have found within them the wisdom and guidance of a trusted friend.

The most important thing to remember about dreams is they are one of the most valuable untapped resources known to mankind. Many songwriters use the power of dreams to help in the crafting of song lyrics or musical scores. Inventors, such as Thomas Edison have reported that dreams help create inventions. Abraham Lincoln had a prophetic dream of his own assassination. Famous writers have been commonly known to receive ideas for their books in dreams.

You can easily learn how to systematically dream intently to help develop your higher senses. Doing so will make every night of sleep a way to expand your sixth sense capabilities.

Systematic Dreaming

The dream state can provide you with the answers to your questions and problems. When you sleep, natural internal changes aid you in sixth sense development. Your defenses are down, your aura loosens, and the universal consciousness opens more easily.

You can begin to focus on dreaming as a sixth sense tool simply by spending about thirty seconds every night before going to bed doing the following. First, close your eyes. Empty your mind of all thoughts and distractions. Breathe deeply through the nose and out through the mouth. As you breathe deeply, fill your being with gratitude to the universal consciousness. Next, focus your attention at the top of your head, at the crown chakra. When you feel ready, move your focus to your solar plexus. As you feel a state of relaxation and heightened aware-ness, clearly state your intention. Do you have a specific question on which you need guidance? If so, state it. Be very specific with the request. Once you make the request, put it out of your mind. Next, ask that the dream be vivid enough for you to remember. Upon waking, write down the first thoughts that come to you, even if they don't im-mediately appear related. The details could be symbolic, like a puzzle that needs to be put together. If the dream does not provide you with answers, guidance, or even a helping clue, simply repeat the request every night. An answer will surely come.

Use knowledge from your own life to interpret the meanings of your dreams. Don't rely too heavily on dream interpretation books because their explanations of dream symbols are often too general to include the specific cir-cumstances of your own life. If you are really stumped about a dream's meaning, dream dictionaries may be a good starting point to get you thinking about a pos-sible meaning, but if you consistently depend on these books to interpret your dreams you may be avoiding a true wealth of information—your own thoughts, feelings, and experiences.

What's Better for Lucid Dreaming: Nighttime Sleep or Daytime Napping?

Some people wonder whether daytime sleep, such as a nap, or nighttime sleep are the same for receiving messages through dreams. In my opinion, nighttime sleep is far superior for sixth sense dreaming. The dark, quiet atmosphere of the night, along with cooler temperatures, act as a conduit for sixth sense energy to flow. The best time for lucid dreaming is dawn, when night turns into day. Most prophetic dreams and dreams of deceased loved ones take place during this time of daily renewal. Dreams that take place at or around dawn also contain the most memorable, reliable, and accurate information. If a person has a stunning dream that affected them so deeply they never forgot it or a dream that gives them goose bumps when recalling it, in all likelihood the dream occurred at or near dawn.

Write It All Down

When I first began working with prophetic dreams, the dreams were simplistic and few and far between. I also spent much more time than I do now in trying to interpret them. As the years progressed, the information I receive through dreams has become more and more complex. The dreams are shorter, but loaded with symbolism and detail. Any future events predicted in the dreams now have much more accuracy in their content, timing, and outcome. As you progress with dream development, you may notice your dreams' details changing as well. Over time, your dreams may change from simplistic and a bit chaotic in their message delivery, to being shorter and loaded with much more relevant symbolism and detail.

As with any other learning experience, the better you get at remembering, recording, and referring back to your dream information, the faster your progress. In the chapter, "Keep Journals," you will be guided, for example, on how to record a dream's content. I suggest you keep this information as your reference guide, add to it constantly, and review the contents periodically to find patterns and symbols. Patterns may occur in timing. Symbols may occur to prepare you for the good times to come. Symbols may also warn you to refrain from action or they may cushion the impact of life's negative events. Watch for set time periods from the time you have the dream to the time the dream manifests. For some, events happen within a few days, for others it could be weeks or months. For a major life change prediction, manifestation of the dream could take years.

Now that we have the basics, let's move forward with four examples that will help illustrate the concept of the unlimited potential and power of dreams.

Dream 1: Black Cat Bad Luck or New Cat to Love?

This simple example will illustrate how important it is to use your common sense, be confident, and trust yourself to determine the meaning of your own dreams and not someone else's interpretation.

I had a repetitive dream about five years ago of a black cat walking up to my front door and waiting for it to open. I had this same dream many times for several weeks. The only difference I noted about the dream was close to the last time I dreamed it—I saw myself opening the door to let the black cat into the house.

If I based the dream interpretation on anecdotal information or if I used a dream interpretation book to analyze its meaning, I may arrive at the wrong explanation as set forth below:

In the dream, the front door of my home symbolizes the good and the bad experiences that flow in and out of my life. The front door as depicted is identical to the actual front door of my home; therefore, I have to take careful notice of this dream, as it is something that is going to happen specifically to me.

Now let's look at the meaning of the black cat staring at the door. Cats throughout history have been related to luck. Black cats are related to bad luck.

When I first began having this repetitive dream,

my front door was closed and the cat just sat and stared at the door. The cat—and therefore the luck, is purposely directed at me. Since I am the one who opened the door, I am now opening the door to bad luck entering my life. I need to be prepared for something bad that I am allowing into my life. It is coming my way very soon.

From all the work I've done on dreams throughout the years, I knew, first of all, the above interpretation was wrong. This dream was not a symbolic dream. There was no bad luck coming. I had no bad gut feeling about the dream and the black cat is not on my list of personal symbols of bad luck or difficult times coming. But, if this dream is not a symbolic one, what is it? The dream was a *literal prediction* dream. There was no symbolism here. The dream literally meant a stray black cat was watching my house and really wanted to live there. He was watching my every move. He was probably also noticing there were no other cats in the house. He may also have sensed my love for animals. This particular cat was really focusing on me and my home. He would soon be making a move to get closer until he moved in permanently.

Just as the dream predicted, a little black cat *did* make an appearance. The new cat, Bella, became a welcomed member of the household. The dream, for me, was not a bad luck dream, but a literal, prophetic one telling me a new pet was in my future.

Dream 2: Warning. Warning. Warning.

I had another recurring dream whose meaning was not as sweet as the first dream. Many years ago, I had begun to teach in the evening at a local school. I loved the school, my students, and the subject matter. Every night for over a month from the time I started to teach, I had the same dream. The dream was so disturbing, it got to the point where I didn't want to sleep. Each night I purposely propped myself up in bed with pillows to allow me to rest, but not fall completely asleep—I couldn't bear to have the horrible dream one more time. Unfortunately, no matter how hard I tried to stay awake, I would always fall asleep and have the same dream.

In the dream, I was dressed in the same clothing I wore when I taught my class. I was holding my briefcase in one hand and my books in the other. I left my classroom and walked down a staircase toward the schools' basement. The walls were tiled, but they looked old and dirty. The lighting was dreary, and there were shadows all around. The time seemed to be late in the evening. As I continued to walk, I passed a small closet. The closet door swung open. I was pulled into the closet, which immediately became a huge, transparent, square container of water. The container of water became very large, maybe ten feet high and ten feet wide. I was struggling in the container of water with every last bit of strength to get out. No matter how hard I tried, I could not get out. I caught a glimpse of a dark shadow of a man watching my struggle. He was on the outside of the container, watching me drown. I could actually feel my lungs filling with water, and the inability to breathe. As the life force left me, I would literally wake up from the dream choking and gasping for air. The dream's physical events left me exhausted.

I had the same dream every night without variation for weeks. The detail and repetition were frightening in and of themselves, but what was most disturbing was my body felt every stage of the struggle and drowning. I knew I was in some type of great danger that was soon to come.

I decided to begin my dream interpretation by reviewing everything I did and every place I went throughout my week. The dream was accurate, placing me in the school where I had just started to teach. I taught in the evening and concluded my class at 9:30 PM. I was always the last person to leave the classroom because I always remained to answer any questions the students had. When the last student left, I closed up the classroom and walked out alone; almost everyone was gone by the time I left. I realized there was a pattern to my exit—I always walked down the three flights of stairs into the school's basement. I walked past the faculty dining room, a small restroom, and out the door to the parking lot. I chose this route because it was a shortcut out of the building. As I focused more and more on the details of the dream, I remembered noticing the same small group of men loitering near the area of my exit. Their presence was a bit unnerving, as I would see them "in the shadows" not performing any work duties, but just standing around.

The dream's meaning now became very clear. The dream was a *prophetic warning* dream. Someone was watching me and I was in danger. The danger was focused at the closet that I walked past. I could easily have been the victim of an assault and even death, because in the dream, I could sense the life force clearly leaving my body and the feeling of drowning. Once I discovered the dream's true meaning and changed my actions (my exit route out of the building), I never had this dream again, likely because I changed my fate.

Prophetic warning dreams are always a call to action. You are given the time and opportunity to change your destiny. I heeded the advice by just changing my exit route from the building. Never having a dream again after you've made some kind of change is important verification of a prophetic warning dream.

As a postscript to the story, I heard through the grape vine shortly thereafter that one of the men who worked there was fired for "bothering someone." I am sorry for whoever he bothered, but I'm glad the danger didn't become a reality for me.

Dream 3: Career Counseling by the Dead

I had just completed my MBA and was applying to the Ph.D. program in marketing at a nearby university. I was an assistant professor at the time, and needed an additional advanced degree to continue with my academic career. Although this particular program did not feel like a good fit for me, I decided to go through with it anyway. I set aside a Saturday to complete the extensive application. It was very late in the evening when I finished, but I wanted to feel like it was on its way and out of my hands. I took the application directly to the post office and deposited it in the outside mailbox. I returned home and, because I was so exhausted, went directly to bed. I had no idea of what was to follow.

That night, I dreamed of my maternal grandfather. Probably not a big deal for most, but for me it was astonishing—I had never met him. He died almost ten years before I was born. I recognized him from the wedding picture of him and my grandmother that always sat on my mother's dresser.

I will never forget this dream. It began with Grandpop and I walking side by side in a beautiful park. The green color of the grass and bushes was the brightest, purest color I had ever seen. It was so beautiful that it was almost indescribable. The paths in the park were winding. There were hills of all sizes and shapes in the distance. Even though the park was large, no one but Grandpop and I were there. He then asked me to sit with him on a bench. I slowly sat down, but all the while I couldn't take my eyes off of him, not even for a moment. Grandpop looked identical to how he looked in the wedding picture, even with his round glasses. He had a glow, almost like a deity. I experienced a sense of awe in his presence. Grandpop told me to forget the Ph.D. program. Even though I'd get the degree, it would never help me on my life's path. What I needed, he said, was an education that would develop who I was inside of me, my true essence. I needed to do that not only for me, but also for others. He told me that by going to law school that would happen. He gave me step-by-step directions, including which university's law school would be best. The school would be open tomorrow. There would be a bin with one catalog and one application. The catalog had a torn cover. Both the catalog and application would be upside down in the and industry contacts. Needless to say, we were stuck and there was nothing any of us could do.

The big problem in this particular case was the sellers needed all their money to settle on their new house. Without the money, the deal would end. In addition to losing out on their new home, the possibility of lawsuits for defaulting on their contract was very likely.

After weeks of trying to get the deal through, one night I asked for help before I went to sleep. What could it hurt? We were at a total dead end. In a dream, the name of a mortgage company in the tertiary market totally unrelated to this transaction came clearly to me. I trusted the information as a clue to move things along, and I immediately acted on it. I called my contact at that company and explained the situation. Within minutes, he was able to direct me to the person who could give me what I needed for settlement purposes the next day. The deal went through. The clients received all their money at the settlement table because nothing needed to be escrowed. The title people were happy, I was elated, and the clients were thrilled.

Begin today to practice systematic dreaming and tap in to the infinite power of dreams as a sixth sense development tool. Dreams are the greatest free natural resource known to humans. Trust their guidance and wisdom.

bin. He cautioned me that I didn't have much time, and that I should act on it now. With that, the dream ended.

I woke up stunned, and ran to wake my mother up to tell her every detail of the dream. As I did, her face showed shock and disbelief. She could not believe I had direct contact with her dad, who had died decades earlier. In fact, she set out to try to trick me. The following conversation ensued:

Mother: Did he talk to you in the dream?
Me: Yes, he spoke to me at length.
Mother: In English?
Me: Yes.
Mother: Was his heavy Italian accent very difficult to understand?
Me: No. (I laughed.) In fact the funny thing was his English was perfect with a New England accent.

My mother gasped. I couldn't have been more accurate. She told me he spoke perfect English, with no Italian accent, but with what could best be called a Boston accent, even though he never traveled further north than New York. My mother was convinced I really did have contact with her dad. She told me how wise he always was and said I should listen to his advice. I did.

As a postscript to the dream, I dressed and drove to the law school as he instructed. Remember, it was a Sunday morning around eight. The law school classrooms are contained within the huge law library. The library itself is open twenty-four hours a day, seven days a week. When I got there, it was pouring rain. Luckily, I was able to park out front and walk right in. I asked the librarian at the front desk the location of the admissions office, but was told no one was available and there weren't any catalogs left because the time to apply was about to end. I dismissed his warnings and headed toward the office. As I was getting closer, my heart was pounding and my hands were shaking. As I approached the admissions office, I saw the application bin. It was outside the admissions office next to the director's door. There was only one catalog left and it was turned upside down, the cover torn in half. Underneath was an application form that had been pulled out of the catalog—exactly as Grandpop described it! The synchronicity around the law school application process was unbelievable. I worked frantically to get the application in on time and to take the LSAT. Grandpop was 100 percent correct. Getting my law degree was the best career decision I ever made.

I only dreamed one other time of Grandpop. It was six months before my mother died. He and my maternal grandmother came to me and thanked me for taking care of their daughter. When I woke up, I had the worst feeling in my gut because I knew my mom's end was near.

Dream 4: A House Settlement From Beyond

I was handling the sale of a property that had one problem after the other. The biggest obstacle was not being able to get a "satisfaction letter" from a mortgage company that had been paid in full decades earlier, but had never recorded the proper document in the county deed's office. The company had been bought out by another company decades before and was now out of business. Account numbers had changed continuously, the succession of mortgage companies after that were almost too hard to follow, and many were defunct. When it looked like we had solved things, we hit a brick wall. Without the satisfaction letter, the sellers would have countless problems, such as to either pay a large sum of money out-of-pocket to get the settlement through or leave the money in escrow until they could petition the court for its release. Everyone hit an impasse. Although needing satisfaction letters for old mortgages is actually a very common problem in real estate sales and very easily solved, no on working on this case—from the real estate agent to the t clerk—had ever dealt with anything quite like this be Everyone working on it had lots of experience, know

Energy

I consider the topic of this chapter to be one of the most important for sixth sense development. At the very foundation of your higher sense development, you must understand the mystical concept that everything and everyone, seen or unseen, are energy. Once you change your thinking to perceive all creation as energy, your sixth sense abilities will advance dramatically.

This chapter is divided into three parts. We begin with a discussion of categories of energy where we view all creation as energy. We then move the focus to major energy transitions—birth and death. Universal, being, and imprinted energy will also be discussed with the majority of focus and examples on imprinted energy. We focus on imprinted energy because it is so common and because its presence can have a strong positive or negative effect on your energy field.

Categories of Energy

Energy can be regarded as heavy or light, fast or slow moving, orderly or confused, positive or negative, physical or nonphysical, seen or unseen, and male or female, but the list of energetic descriptions does not end there. As you become more perceptive about energy, your descriptions of it will become more pointed and refined. Of course, more than one word can be used to describe energy. For example, a man can have a strong, masculine, fast-moving, chaotic energy, and a woman can have slow moving, delicate energy.

Now that you can describe all things in terms of energy, take the concept one step further and ponder the strongest energy transitions we experience as humans. Such transitions are how we spiritually come into this world and how we spiritually leave. There are many thoughts and theories in philosophy, religion, mystical studies, and even among individuals on how energy enters the body at birth and how it exits the body at death.

Energetic Thoughts on Birth and Death

Some believe the life force enters the body at birth through the top of the head. Others believe the life force enters the body through the solar plexus. Some believe life enters through the hands, others believe the point of entry is the feet, and still others believe the nose or mouth is where life force enters the body. The theories are myriad, so let's move on to transition by death.

Some believe at death the life force exits the body through the hands or through the feet; others believe life exits through the solar plexus; others believe the exit is through the top of the head; some say it is through the nose or mouth; while others believe the entire being in spirit form just moves aside from the physical body, leaving the physical existence behind. Again, there are so many different beliefs on this subject. Of course, there are those who say when we die the life force literally dissolves because there is no spirit to go anywhere. For our purposes, we won't be entertaining the "no spirit" concept.

The debate on the entrance and exit of energy at birth and death may never be resolved, but we can count on two things. First, the theories will remain controversial and be the subject of philosophy, religion, mystical studies, and our own informal pondering for many years to come. Second, we may all agree the energy exchange between dimensions is dramatic for one being born and for one dying. But what about the effect the energy exchanges have on the newly born or newly deceased's closest loved ones?

Energy of Birth

When someone is born, a dramatic energetic effect occurs. First, there is an energy exchange from a lighter dimension to a heavier one. Additional energy is entering a contained energy field known as the family unit. The family unit can be composed of one or more persons. The energy entering that contained energy field has all kinds of energetic consequences. Second, sometimes the energy of the new arrival is so strong that a more weakened member of the family unit may pass away shortly before or shortly after the birth. The death can be thought of as an energetic balance to the energy of the family unit. Whatever the qualities, the new energy will have its own effects for years to come.

Energy of Death

Let us now change gears and focus on the energetic events surrounding death. At the moment of death, the energy exchange between dimensions is very drastic. When someone dies, the so-called "life force" or "life energy" moves from our heavy material world to the faster-moving unseen world. Some people who have had life after life experiences describe the transition as feeling like they are being sucked into a vacuum tube. What is experienced is the strong energy exchange between dimensions, also known as the transition. If instead of dying they return to their physical body, some survivors have recounted feeling and hearing what could best be described as a *thud*. The sound was their worldly attempt to describe what seemed to be an energy jolt forcing the life energy back into the body, and therefore, back into the third dimension.

It's interesting to note that in addition to the drastic energy exchange of the person transitioning, if you have a close relationship with someone who has died, not only do you have to cope with your feelings of grief and the negative impact of their death on your life, you also temporarily have to deal with an unseen problem. Without you consciously knowing it, you have to emotionally manage the effect that the deceased's transitional energy has on your own energy field.

When you feel a heart-felt closeness to someone either through family relations or a close friendship, the energies of both your spiritual bodies are literally tied to each other. That is why people readily get premonitions about something bad happening to those they love. Both energies are literally wrapped around each other.

When someone very close to us dies, we feel more than just sadness. In addition to our grief, we experience the person's death as an energy exchange. This happens without us consciously understanding what is going on.

One of the most common ways people experience this energy connection is by having what I call the "death dream." The death dream is the first dream of the deceased occurring shortly after their death, usually within one to three days. In that dream, the deceased is usually seen radiantly smiling. Many times, the person's eyes are sky blue, even if blue was not their eye color in this life. The person's radiant smile and eye color tells you he or she is alive, well, happy, strong, and basking in love and wisdom. The deceased can be completely alone or with others in the dream. Either way, the message tells you they made the journey home safely and are happy.

In addition to the death dream, there is another type of contact with the deceased. If the deceased did not fully transition to the light after death, the deceased's energy attaches to the energy field of his or her closest living loved one (or ones). Most people don't feel the attachment, but for those who do, the feeling is an unexplained discomfort or energy presence. Normally the feeling is physically felt around the shoulders, above the head, or directly behind the body. Some may feel what can best be described as "energetic turbulence" or energy swirling in and around their body. They may feel like clouds floating above and around their head. The energy attachment can be so strong that it can cause dizziness. Whatever the description, what is being experienced is the energy attachment of the deceased's energy to the energy field of the living.

The attachment is normally temporary, only lasting until the deceased makes the full transition to the light, moving on with their spiritual journey. Attachments can be initiated by the deceased or the living. When the deceased form attachments, they do so mainly for three reasons. First, if the deceased passed on with numerous or excessively urgent worries about those left behind, they may not be able to fully transition. They energetically "hang on" to those they are worried about leaving. Second, if the death was sudden and unnatural in any way (such as by accident, homicide, or suicide), the body, mind, and spirit couldn't properly reconcile the energy transition and need time to do so; therefore, an attachment takes place. Third, if there was unfinished business between the deceased, such as something that needed to be said or done, an energetic attachment could form.

The deceased is not the only one who creates attachments, however. When mourners grieve continuously and cry out for the deceased well after a healthy amount of time has passed, their strong thoughts lock much of the deceased's energy in the third dimension. The deceased's spiritual transition is put on hold because the heaviness of the third dimension, in conjunction with the heaviness of the loved one's thoughts, act as an anchor that holds them back spiritually. Please remember, if you lose a beloved family member or friend, it was divine will. Always keep the deceased in your thoughts and prayers, of course, but move forward with your life's journey. You still have much to do, and the deceased's spirit needs to be free to do its work on the other side.

Energy Tuning Exercise 1

Now that you're beginning to perceive all things as energy and thinking about life and death as major energetic transitions, let's do some energy tuning exercises. We'll begin with experiencing the effect different types of energies have on you.

To become quickly tuned to energy, I want you to do the following exercise *by yourself*. Spend one morning or afternoon on a weekday visiting the following three places in this order: a courthouse, a hospital, and an arboretum or park. You only have to spend thirty minutes to one hour in each place, but don't go over one hour. I want you to do this exercise on a weekday for practical reasons. On the weekend, the courthouse may be closed. As for the hospital, the more calming energy of additional visitors during the weekend will level out the overall intense energy experience I want you to have. The arboretum or park will be more crowded on the weekend resulting in you getting more "people energy" instead of the full energetic plant experience.

No one should accompany you on this exercise for two reasons: first, there should be minimal distractions; and second, if you bring someone with, you both will compare and contrast your feelings. Even if you agree not to discuss the exercises until the end, just being together dilutes the energetic experience. Get the most out of the exercise by doing it on your own. Be sure to turn off your cell phone. Don't bring any music player or any other distractions. Clear the mind of thoughts and distractions because you have to focus intently. You will need a pad of paper and a pen. You can repeat the exercise as many times as you wish, but if you are focused and very sensitive, you only need to do it once for its full impact to be deeply felt.

1. *The Courthouse*. As you physically approach the courthouse, focus on the energy you feel in and around you. Walk into the courthouse. Do not focus on any particular person in the courthouse, otherwise you will get confused and distracted by individual energy. Focus on the overall energy. Walk around the halls of the courthouse and spend a few minutes in a courtroom open to the public, even if it's empty. What does the energy feel like? Does the energy make you feel tense?

Record how the courtroom energetically feels and if there is any energetic affect on you physically, emotionally, and/or spiritually. Do not rationalize or try to explain your feelings. Just experience your feelings as they come and record them in detail.

2. **The Hospital.** Leave the courthouse and go directly to a hospital. Try not to think about your feelings related to the courthouse as you travel to the hospital. Center yourself. As you get physically close to the hospital, note how you feel energetically. Enter the hospital and go to energy-intense locations such as the emergency room, the post-op waiting room, and the chemotherapy waiting room. How does it *energetically* feel in these places? How does the energy of these places affect you? Do you, for example, feel fear? If you feel fear, where does your body record it? Do you feel sick to your stomach, or do you feel chills in your extremities? Maybe you physically feel nothing. Maybe you just feel emotionally drained or very apprehensive. Pay very careful attention and record how you feel physically and emotionally.

3. **The Arboretum or Park.** Once you leave the hospital, travel to an arboretum or park. Center

yourself and record how you energetically feel as you approach either of the two. Do not think about the prior two places. Just focus on how you energetically feel being physically near and around all the plants. What is the physical and/or emotional effect the plants have on you?

When you finish the entire exercise of visiting all three places, you should feel two things. First, you should feel tired from all the extreme energetic differences you experienced. If you aren't tired at the end of the exercise, you might not yet be energetically sensitive enough, or you didn't open and focus as intensely as you should have. Also, if you only slightly felt differences in energy in the three places, you need to sensitize yourself more to energy by spending more quiet time centering yourself, breathing deeply, and emptying the mind of all thoughts. When you've done so, repeat the exercise. Feel the differences in energy.

If you work at any of these places, you may not feel the impact of this exercise; therefore, substitute another similar high-impact environment for whichever one you are employed.

Energy Tuning Exercise 2

You may also want to try an energy exercise at home. I call it the "home energy observation." This one is easy and quick to do. First, center yourself through deep breathing and emptying the mind of thoughts and distractions. When no one is home, go into each room of your home after dark. Try not to turn on a light because without light, it is easier to focus on the room's energetic feeling. By looking at a furnished room, the focus will be on the physicality and not on the energy. Try to find a chair in each room and sit quietly for a few minutes. Think of what each room energetically feels like. As an example, you should feel an energetic burst of youthfulness, contentment, newness, or high energy coming from a child's bedroom or playroom. That energy should put a smile on your face. On the contrary, a storage room and an attic may give off a slight (or not so slight) feeling of stagnation or confusion. If teenaged sons or daughters are giving you problems, you should be able to feel the energy of unrest or turmoil in their bedrooms. Home energy observation exercise is a good one to do because your home is an energetic extension of you. It is a great energetic "home monitor;" in other words, if all feels fine on the "home front," things should be doing well in your life. If you energetically feel the opposite, such as walking into any of the rooms and feeling sad, confused, or unable to relax, you need to do work on the home, but especially on yourself and the family member who inhabits that room.

Now that you are thinking of everything as energy, let us move to what I consider the three types of energy you will encounter in your sixth sense development. They are universal energy, being energy, and imprinted energy. My three-part energy simplification should help you maintain your focus and improve your sixth sense development without much effort.

Universal Energy

Let's begin with universal energy. Universal energy is composed of infinite love and wisdom. You can receive universal energy through any of your senses. Dreams are also a great conduit of universal energy. Inspiration or any form of creativity, for example, makes its way to you through universal energy. Ideas that come from universal energy are usually worth pursuing because they come from a higher force and are sent to you to guide you on your journey. Be aware of the wealth of energy available via the universe.

Being Energy

The second type of energy is what I term "being energy." Being energy is energy received from any living form or being in the universe. Beings are made up of spirit, and include people, animals, plants, and even rocks and stones. Begin to be very aware of energy that emanates from every type of being you encounter.

Repeat the Special Person (SP) exercise from the "Awareness" chapter by thinking about the person you most love. Feel your energy react as you think of this special person. By thinking of your special person, you should feel your heart melt. What you are experiencing is being energy influencing your own energy system. You can have the same "being experience" with a beloved pet. Any being can evoke intense positive or negative energetic feelings in you.

Imprinted Energy

The last type of energy we will discuss is imprinted energy. Imprinted energy is at times the most complex and difficult energy to understand. I am devoting more discussion to imprinted energy than the other two types because by understanding imprinted energy, your sixth sense will more easily deepen.

Imprinted energy is just that—energy that comes in contact with a thing or a place and imprints its energy upon it. The information that comes to you as imprinted energy can come through any of the senses. Accept the imprinted energy's information without any analysis.

Imprinted energy can be positive or negative. Positive imprinted energy is uplifting. Negative imprinted energy, on the other hand, needs discussion as it is very intense, and we'll be using it as a learning tool. There are two important elements of negative imprinted energy of which to be aware.

In Part I of this book, we spoke of clairtangency and psychometry. Without imprinted energy, you cannot practice psychometry—otherwise there wouldn't be anything left to read or absorb.

First, negative imprinted energy adversely affects people in unimaginable ways. It can manifest in a person as a physical and/or emotional ailment. Negative imprinted energy can create dissent in a household. Household members may start arguments with one another for no apparent reason. They may experience unexplained headaches, aches and pains, general fatigue, depression, dissatisfaction with life, insomnia, irritability, and all kinds of difficult-to-diagnose ailments. If the ailments are difficult to diagnose and their onset was around the time the people moved into a new home, the most likely cause is from imprinted negative energy. Each person's reaction to negativity is different.

Years ago when marriages were failing, the most often-given advice was to move, for things would change (before filing for divorce). There's actually a lot of truth to that advice—if the imprinted energy manifested as unrest, anxiety, and general unhappiness, a couple taken out of that environment could very likely see their marriage improve.

Another thing to know about negative imprinted energy is that it remains until something is done to stop it. Remember old phonographic records? They used to get flaws or skips in them when they were played too much, resulting in the same words or music being heard over and over until someone either moved the needle or turned the machine off. Imprinted energy acts the same way. It just keeps repeating itself over and over until something is done consciously or unconsciously to remove it.

Let's do a quick exercise in imprinted energy. In your hand, hold any item that someone else owns or owned, especially something they often had direct contact with, such as keys. Pick up the item and focus on what comes to you from the imprinted energy the owner has left behind. Do you feel happiness, sadness, or indifference? Be open to whatever comes through the senses. Actually, the best place to practice the receipt of imprinted energy is at a flea market. Touch or hold any item for sale and be open to your impressions. The flea market is a great testing ground because you do not know who the former owners of the items were, making you open to whatever impressions come forth. Let's assume you bought an old desk at a flea market. When you take the desk home to use it, you may sense something about its previous owner. You may sense that a very intelligent man studied late at night at the desk for many years. What you're feeling is the imprinted energy left by the previous owner. If at the flea market you feel like setting an item down because the imprinted energy doesn't feel right, do so. The imprinted energy isn't compatible with yours.

Energy can attach not only to things, but also to places. Energy can attach to a place as a result of an event that happened there. The place becomes like a photographic negative absorbing the energy of the event or events. If there was an explosion or an accident on a particular piece of land you're standing on, you may be able to intuitively feel the chaos or destruction of the explosion or accident.

Information from imprinted energy can be perceived through any of your senses. If you visit a cemetery, for example, you may be able to hear by clairaudience, or feel by clairsentience the sobbing of mourners. The emotions might be so strong that the sound of the mourners become imprinted or absorbed by the land there itself. The sounds could actually be many years old, but on a higher energy vibration level that is locked in this location. Whether we are able to hear them or not, the sounds play over and over again. An example of this phenomenon can be found in Normandy, France. Many people, even those without heightened senses, visit where the battle of Normandy took place and come away feeling as if the battle is still going on. They claim to hear the sounds of war and feel the trauma. What is being felt is the horrific imprinted energy that was absorbed in the ground.

Many times, imprinted energy remains long after changes are made to a place. For example, a cemetery may become a housing development, but the feelings of the mourners remain imprinted.

A very negative and dramatic example of imprinted energy, and one worth discussing as a learning concept, is the energy of murder. A murder is the unnatural ending of another's life force. Murder takes place against the laws of nature. The struggle to stay alive and the loss of the life battle remain in the place where it happened. Let us take the example of a murder that occurred in a particular room in a house. The room and even the entire house absorb the trauma. If an energetically sensitive person enters that room, that person will immediately feel uneasy and want to leave. If the person entering the room has advanced heightened senses, he or she could actually see the murder taking place, the perpetrator, the victim, and the aftermath through the mind's eye. In addition to seeing the event unfold, the person with heightened senses many times also experiences the emotional and physical trauma of the victim in their own body.

Imprinted Energy Comes Alive

Here's one of my own experiences with imprinted energy. I had just started graduate school and met a new friend, Pam. Pam loved to talk about her family, especially her dad, a doctor, whom she admired very much. Pam's eyes would light up as she talked about all the people whose lives he touched in so many good ways. One day after class, Pam and I were driving past her dad's office and we decided to visit him. As we pulled up, I was surprised by the structure. The office was an old house, not the usual commercial office building.

After we entered the building and said hi to her dad and the staff, Pam took me for a tour upstairs because it was, in her words, "so cool up there."

Pam told me the second floor wasn't renovated and seemed to be the living quarters of many years ago when the building was a residence. As we walked up the stairs, I had no idea I was in for a very unpleasant surprise.

We began our tour of the second floor by going into the master bedroom, and then into a smaller bedroom. Both rooms were used for storing old patient files and unused office supplies. We then walked to the bedroom Pam claimed was always cold, even on the hottest and most humid days in summer. As I walked in, the imprinted energy immediately came alive and I absorbed it all. My breathing became rapid and shallow. I had trouble swallowing. I felt sick and shocked as I watched in horror a little girl being murdered. Her lifeless body was thrown at the wall and slowly fell to the floor. I turned to Pam and said, "Let's get out of here." As we left, I told her what happened in the few seconds we were in that room. Her eyes filled with tears as she told me a very sad story. According to Pam, a young family with a girl about four years old lived in the house decades ago. The little girl was killed in that very same room and her murderer was never found. The family was so distraught, they could no longer live there, and so left. Through the years, the property had many owners. It seemed no one could live there for more than a few years at a time, and it wasn't surprising Pam's father paid very little for the house.

I wish Pam had told me the history surrounding the house, and the history of that particular bedroom before we went to visit! If I had known, I would have stayed home and saved myself lots of stress. As a postscript to the story, after Pam's father retired, the property burned down to the ground. It seems that only intense fire could balance that horrible energy vibe.

Here's another example of imprinted energy. Many years ago, my friend Dave had to drop off an art school project at his teacher's house. Dave was only going to stop for a minute, so I said I would ride with him and wait in the car as he spoke to his teacher. As luck would have it, the teacher wanted to talk to him for a while. Dave asked me to come in and sit down as I would be more comfortable inside. As I sat down in one of the teacher's chairs, the show began. I immediately saw dogs and cats of all shapes and sizes lined up, shaking with fright. My heart started to pound, my pulse raced out of control, and my breathing became very shallow. I felt very sick to my stomach and wanted to run out of there and never return. I remained frozen in place until it was time to leave. When we got outside, I asked Dave if he knew the house was a veterinarian office before his teacher moved in. He said he didn't know but he would ask his teacher when he returned to school the following week. Lo and behold, just as I had said, the house was formerly a veterinarian office for many years before it was converted to a residence. The imprinted energy of fear was locked in that house. In this case, imprinted energy manifested in strange ways. The teacher and his spouse could not understand the origin of the constant anxiety and nervousness experienced by their children since moving into their "dream home." No matter what the parents tried to do to alleviate the anxiety, nothing helped. Nothing would help because the problem wasn't the children, it was the imprinted energy.

Although all the imprinted energy examples here were negative, I want to stress that imprinted energy can also be positive. My present law office used to be a child's clothing store, and the imprinted energy of children frequently entering the store remains as a very good and uplifting feeling in the office. The imprinted energy of my former law office was much different—that office used to be a speakeasy and gambling hall. Sometimes, late in the day when clients left and the rooms were quiet, you could literally hear a party going on! You could feel the energy of many people present. Office employees often spoke of smelling cigarette smoke and alcoholic beverages. Whenever we hired a new employee to work after hours, we would all find it humorous to hear what the new hire had to say. Without fail, all spoke of how "creepy" it was to work there at night. All felt the same feeling of people peering over their shoulders to glance at their work.

Practice your energy perception abilities every day and take special notice of its impact on your physical, emotional, and spiritual bodies.

Freedom

The preceding chapter focused on all kinds of energy you can encounter throughout your day and even your lifetime. This chapter, entitled Freedom, is a sixth sense development tool I consider the twin of energy. Freedom, as the term is used here, keeps the door of sixth sense gifts and abilities swinging wide open. As I use it in this book, freedom pertains to healthy maintenance of the energy field, keeping it free from negative attachments. How do we perform such maintenance? Using easy, natural, and uncomplicated external remedies.

The Aura or Energy Field

The aura or energy field is a living, breathing energy field, a part and extension of you. The aura acts like a magnet, constantly attracting and repelling all kinds of energy, positive or negative. Energy attraction occurs continuously from the time you are born until the time you die.

Not all the energy you attract is desirable. Because the energy field acts like a magnet, both desirable and undesirable energy can be trapped in the energy field. The problem is not the desirable energy. It is the undesirable energy that needs to be repelled and released. Any unwanted negative energy that remains adversely affects one's physical, emotional, and spiritual health, including sixth sense development. You want your energy field or aura to be clear of as much outside energy as you can so it can freely function and evolve on its own.

When the aura is strong it circulates with a healthy rhythm around the body. It has few "bits" of unwanted, negative energy and remains free to support developing the higher senses. In addition, when the energy field is free from unwanted attachments, the aura's colors are beautiful and vibrant. Like everything else, the aura functions with its own yin and yang characteristics. It breathes in its own way by expanding and contracting. When expanding, the aura opens itself to the universal consciousness. A healthy aura is a beautiful thing to behold—it works in rhythm with nature and helps attract what is good and wholesome into your life. You cannot have true sixth sense development without the energy field or aura freely functioning at peak performance.

Freedom Through Nature

Let's begin our methods of gaining energy freedom with the most basic one—go outdoors and commune with nature. Ideally, communing with nature should be done every day for at least an hour, but at a minimum, you should have contact with nature at least once a week. I recommend a walk in the park. When you are in the park, you breathe in fresh air; look up at the sky; walk directly on the grass; and surround yourself with trees, plants, and many of God's creatures.

Communing with nature allows you the opportunity to absorb nature through all your senses. Don't do what most people do when they take a walk—that is, recount your day or review a problem. To practice true freedom as a sixth sense development tool, use the time during a nature walk to disconnect from the events of the day and your troubles. As your walk, empty your mind and breathe deeply. Look at the earth's bounty. Focus on the trees, flowers, and bushes. Look at the animals running free, and the insects and birds flying by. If there is no park nearby, walk along a lake, the seashore, or any body of water. If there aren't any parks or bodies of water near you, at least walk where there are some trees. You may wish to lean against a large, strong tree and energetically feel its size and strength. Next, focus on the sky with its cloud formations, its vastness ,and its beauty. Fill your senses with thoughts of total energy freedom around you. Fill your heart with a sense of gratitude for the energetic disconnection from unwanted negative energy released from your aura. Your energy field will automatically absorb the much needed energy from nature, helping to strengthen, cleanse, and revitalize your energy field.

Oils

Another method to gain freedom for the energy field is by using a citrus spritz. Purchase a small bottle (one ounce) of pure citrus oil. Purchase the oil from a health food store and make sure the oil is 100 percent natural. Do not use manufactured sweet smelling perfumes or colognes, as they contain other chemicals not conducive to the natural state we wish to reach. Pour the contents of the bottle into a small spray bottle. Add one pint of pure spring water. Very lightly spray the contents of the bottle on and around your body, like you would with cologne. You can do this anytime you wish to free the aura of unwanted negative energy attaching itself to your energy field. The oil's freshness and vitality will give an immediate temporary lift from the heaviness or darkness that has attached to you.

Sea Salt

Sometimes the negativity you absorb in your energy field is so strong that it takes away most of your positive outlook, and leaves you weakened or in a state of pessimistic thought. You may have had one of "those days" (or weeks) where everything has gone wrong. In that case, you will need more than a walk outside or a quick spray of citrus oil. To counteract such strong negativity, I recommend you take a "sea salt shower." To do a sea salt shower, purchase a bag of pure sea salt from the health food store. Have a timer ready, set for five to ten minutes. Take your usual shower, but do not get dried. Just stand in the shower and turn off the water. Open the bag of sea salt. Pour a small amount in your hand and begin to apply a thin film of salt all over your body. Apply the salt to the front and back of the neck, front and back of the torso, on all sides of the extremities, and on the front and back of the feet and hands. Avoid putting the sea salt on the head and face. You may require most, if not the entire, bag of salt. Also, some salt will fall on the shower floor. That is fine. Do not expect every grain of salt to stick to you. When you are finished putting the salt all over your body, stand quietly in the shower with the water off. Start the timer. Do not go past ten minutes or the process will have the opposite effect, slightly weakening you. If you let the salt sit for less than five minutes, it won't have time to work.

As you stand in the shower with the sea salt, breathe deeply, empty your mind, and begin to think good thoughts of beautiful vibrant colors surrounding you. Think of your energy field as both expansive and devoid of unwanted attachments. Think also of the beautiful rhythmic energy flowing in and around you. When the time is up, rinse everything. If possible, schedule the salt shower before bedtime for the best and most immediate results.

The day after the salt shower, you will feel stronger and more grounded and optimistic. Your head will be clearer and you will feel ready to face life's difficulties again. As the salt shower is so effective, you should not do it more than once or twice a week. The salt shower has a profound impact on your energy field and sixth sense development because of its balancing powers on the body, mind, and spirit.

Please do not make an appointment with the local salon or spa in hopes their applications may free the aura—it won't happen! You need to do the work yourself along with nature to free the aura of unwanted influences. The spa is a fun place to go, but its affects do not penetrate on a deep spiritual level the way the methods in this chapter will.

Gazing

One of the most mystical activities you can experience is gazing. Gazing is an "unfocused focus" that uses a clear surface as a conduit for receiving visual images from the universal consciousness. Gazing is a hold-over from ancient times. It is a timeless sixth sense tool and one that can be done anywhere and anytime. The ways you can gaze are only limited by your imagination.

How to Gaze

Let's begin with what I consider the five components of gazing.

First, you need a clear surface—it acts as a conduit for focus and quieting of the mind, two things needed for receiving sixth sense messages. Any clear surface will do, such as water in a glass mug, a clear bowl filled with water, a clear quartz crystal of any shape or any size, a mirror, or a clean natural body of water. The type of clear surface you choose is limited only by your imagination.

Second, you must breathe very slowly and deeply for a few minutes before gazing; this will calm and center your mind and body. You should feel relaxed, but alert and aware.

Third, while breathing deeply, close your eyes and empty your mind of all thoughts and distractions.

Fourth, slowly open your eyes and begin to gaze into the clear surface.

Fifth, always have paper and a pen nearby to immediately record everything that comes forth. Believe me, the messages will be forgotten, especially the important details, so write them in a journal devoted just to gazing. More on journals will be discussed in the chapter, "Keep Journals." Include the date, how much time you took to gaze, and your recollection of what you saw. The messages are not easily recalled later because you are literally acting as a conduit or channel through which information is passing. The messages don't necessarily stick and you may easily lose out on information relevant to your life.

To illustrate how gazing works, let's take an example of a water pipe that has no stopper. You are the pipe, the messages are the water, and the stopper is the written record. The messages pass through the pipe. If you put no stopper in the pipe, the water cannot be recouped; it is gone forever. So it is with the messages. Without writing them down, the messages are lost forever. What if you gaze and nothing comes through? You should record in the gazing journal that nothing came through. It's important to record "nothing" because a pattern will emerge. You'll discover patterns, such as a particular time of day, for example, may yield no messages while at other times (possibly more relaxed days such as weekends), the visual information moves through the gazed surface almost nonstop.

The Sixth Sense and Gazing

Gazing, in and of itself, has been known to quicken the development of claircognizance and clairaudience. Gazing may also help if you are really stumped on the answer to a nagging question or problem and no solutions are readily coming forward.

When you gaze, your senses are heightened and your spirit is elevated to receive sixth sense information. You feel a sense of peace and warmth because information is being given to you with love and for your highest good.

Gazing is an art—it takes practice. The images received from gazing happen quickly, as fast as the blink of an eye, which is why you need to be alert and attentive during the session. The process itself can take several attempts before you begin to see colors, words, peoples' faces, animals, flowers, numbers, symbols, or any kind of sixth sense message. Messages may be loaded with symbolism and, like dreams, interpreting them correctly will take time. No matter what images or symbols you receive, make no mistake—the messages and their meanings always have importance to your life.

I hope the following examples of gazing encourage you to start your own routine, as gazing is a very accurate and useful tool!

Steve's Gazing Tools

Steve, a highly intuitive architect, does his best gazing in two different places. The first place is on the New Jersey shore, at a small pond. Water is a great conductor of sixth sense energy. This particular pond has proven to be a very interesting place for Steve to gaze—when he looks into the pond, it is like looking through the third eye directly into another dimension, he says. The natural movement of the water makes it easy for him to lapse into a meditative state. His conscious mind is empty, but his subconscious is on alert. When he gazes, Steve is not thinking of his work, his daily chores, or his worries. He focuses only on the water and he always receives helpful guidance to his problems, similar to what he receives through dreams. Steve prefers gazing to dreaming because he believes through gazing his other higher senses have an opportunity to join in.

Steve does his other best gazing in a certain mirror in his home. The mirror is in the kitchen and angled so nothing is reflected in it (i.e., there are no distractions). The mirror gives him the blankness he needs to focus. As an added benefit, because the mirror is in the kitchen, the nearby water in the pipes acts as a conduit for unseen energy to be more easily transferred. Steve's receipt of information is extremely clear and precise with this particular mirror, as the following example will show.

Steve's Gazing Premonition

About four months before Steve's father died, he was looking in his mirror, and caught sight of the image of a coffin. The coffin was somewhat gray and there was a man in it. The face of the man was turned away. Steve couldn't see who it was, but he knew beyond a doubt that it was his father. Steve knows such images are sent by the universal consciousness to help cushion difficult life-changing events, even in his case, when he knew the end of his clos-est loved one was near.

You can gaze any time you want, for as long and as often as you wish. In addition to its effect on opening the senses, gazing is a great form of meditation. The benefits to sixth sense development from gazing are invaluable, because it promotes a general feeling of well-being, an un-explainable "centeredness," and an opening of the higher sense channels to the universal consciousness.

The 3H's

In this chapter we are going to change gears and use more concrete, tangible tools to develop the sixth sense. The tools are your hands and your head. Combining the three creates the 3H exercise. The hands are used to create heat. The heat is applied to the head, specifically to the forehead at the site of the third eye. Remember, the third eye is a major energy center. As heat is applied, the third eye begins to loosen and open, facilitating sixth sense advancement.

How to Do the 3H Exercise

Find a clean, quiet, organized place. Close any windows nearby to cut off external noise. Turn off any noise, like from a television or radio—it will affect your concentration. When all external distractions are quieted, sit in a straight-back chair. Make an effort to have good posture: place your feet flat on the floor, hands folded on your lap, and keep your chin parallel to the floor. Close your eyes. Breathe deeply and empty the mind of thoughts and distractions. When you feel relaxed, put your hands together as if in prayer, and rub them firmly together for at least fifteen seconds to create heat. While still rubbing the hands together, look upward to facilitate the opening of your mind, body, and spirit to positive and upward flowing energy. Next, take the tips of the fingers of both hands (excluding the thumbs) and quickly tap the forehead in and around the location of the third eye. After about a minute, extend the tapping out to cover the top, sides, and back of the head. The action of the tapping in these areas opens the energy blockages in the head, and extends to opening the blockages in and around the ethereal body that surrounds the head, increasing physical and spiritual circulation. You can start and stop the exercise anytime you wish, but you get the best benefits by doing it upon waking after adequate, restful sleep.

Isabel and the 3H Exercise

Every morning for the last thirty days, Isabel has done the 3H exercise upon awakening. She never misses doing it, even if she oversleeps or is running late for work. Isabel takes three to five minutes to do the exercise and has found it helps center and ground her, while opening her third eye and intuition. Isabel has noticed an increase in helpful intuitive ability and gives all the credit to the 3H exercise—it's the only sixth sense development tool she's used.

The 3H exercise is very powerful and very versatile. You can practice it before focusing on any of the senses you wish to develop, or you can just do it by itself for its own sixth sense benefits.

Intention

If you are truly serious about higher sense development, you need genuine, loving, sixth sense intention. Sixth sense intention keeps you unrestricted in your pursuit of sixth sense advancement for all the good it can bring into your life.

Intention happens when you take a few moments (as often as you wish) to aspire toward, be grateful for, and open yourself to the gift of the heightened senses. Without true intention, I believe your spiritual development is blocked. It is almost as if to "graduate" to advanced sixth sense development, you have to pass the intention "test."

Setting forth your intention means having an unspoken, loving desire to open your entire being—body, mind, and spirit—to sixth sense development. With true intention, your entire essence changes dynamically. The senses open to the all knowing universal consciousness and your entire being is drenched in spiritual love, guidance, and wisdom.

With true intention to open the sixth sense comes the trust and belief in yourself that through your efforts you will receive knowledge in the form of wisdom and guidance from the universal consciousness. As your intention becomes assimilated into your being, you will become more confident in your sixth sense development. You will also become convinced that your skills are highly accurate and reliable.

Depending on how balanced your physical, emotional, and spiritual state is, intention can take place instantaneously or be a lifelong accomplishment. I believe if you are interested enough in your sixth sense development, you are already incorporating loving intention into your life and are well on your spiritual journey.

Intention has a twin—gratitude. As a common practice, when you focus on loving intention to advance the sixth sense, always conclude with thoughts or an attitude of gratitude. Examples of gracious affirmations are "Thank you for allowing me to be a conduit of pure loving knowledge," "Thank you for all the helpful guidance you send me," and "I am forever grateful." You do not always have to think words of gratitude. A bow of the head can say it all, or even a general grateful attitude is enough. Just be consistent and sincere.

The benefits of intention aren't just the opening of the senses, but also a feeling of greater inner peace, strength, and comfort. I believe people who want to develop the sixth sense will be more balanced and open to its vastness if they have within them true loving intention.

Chakras and Intention

The chakra system (as discussed in its own section) is closely tied to intention. For the purpose of establishing intention, I consider the proper functioning of the heart chakra to be paramount, because intention in and of itself means a *loving* intention. The chakra most connected to love is the heart chakra. When the heart chakra is open, clear, and properly functioning, compassion and love pour into and out of the heart, and sixth sense development occurs naturally.

Almost everyone I meet tells me of an unusual or unexplained miracle or wonder that happened to them, affecting forever their life or that of a close loved one. I always view these unexplained positive events as eye openers to true unspoken, loving intention. Read the following example and reflect on whether it's similar to one that may have happened to you.

Inconvenience Keeps Brad Alive

One morning Brad was driving to work along his usual route at the usual time. All at once, he realized he left several financial reports at home. He needed those reports for a meeting later that morning. Brad knew that by returning home he would be caught in rush hour traffic and would surely be late, but he absolutely needed those reports for the data they contained. Brad reluctantly returned home to pick up the items, feeling a little silly but mostly annoyed with his carelessness.

Now on his second drive to work that day, Brad guessed that he might still make it on time, but this time a detour delayed him again! Brad grew very impatient. Now he would surely be late and would be reprimanded by his boss. As luck would have it, the boss was out with the flu and no one knew Brad was late. But the real gift came later that day.

It was not until evening when Brad was watching the day's news that it became clear how significant forgetting those reports was for him. At the exact place and time he would normally take a right turn off the highway onto a heavily trafficked route, a very dangerous six-car pileup had occurred. He would have been there at the exact time. All occupants of the cars were either severely injured or had died. Brad would have been one of them. By returning home, Brad avoided a horrific, multi-car collision.

Brad's eyes filled with tears in gratitude for his safety and in sadness for those who weren't as lucky. He whispered a silent "thank you, God," and vowed to never view such occurrences as annoyances but as likely life savers. Brad often meditates on this experience and views it as a turning point in his spiritual life. Brad has become more open to the higher senses and uses this experience as a springboard to true loving intention.

Take time to think back to your own unusual or unexplained mystical experiences. Everybody has one and everyone's life has changed in some way because of it. Use it as your gateway to true loving intention.

Junk

Just the sound of the word "junk" is a turnoff to most people. It evokes thoughts of what is unproductive, useless, and what takes up much-needed space. The word "junk" should give you an immediate jolt of negative energy.

As the term is used here, junk refers to anything physical or nonphysical that negatively affects the energy field. Junk drains you. Junk wastes your time, thoughts, and space. You need to eliminate or minimize junk from your life. By doing so, you will have greater energetic freedom, allowing positive energy to freely move in and around you.

There are three kinds of junk: junk attitudes, thoughts, and things. I will explain each one with strategies you can use to handle them.

Junk Attitudes

We begin with the people who can be quite difficult and challenging. I refer to nasty attitudes as "junk attitudes." People with junk attitudes make life sad for themselves and annoying and frustrating for us, at best. These difficult people have a strong negative vibe. Sometimes just their presence can make you feel down, and their words frustrate, hurt, annoy, or depress you. Their attitude can sadden what was moments ago a happy day because they enjoy hearing the details of hard luck and negative gossip. Their downward vibe attaches and remains with you, even when you leave their presence. Junk attitudes are not compatible with your own positive energy, as you're on the spiritual path. First, the bad news—junk attitudes and the people who have them are here to stay. However, the good news is that there are ways to handle such people, and ways to make interactions with them more palatable.

Spiritual Strategies to Handle People with Junk Attitudes

If you have constant, unavoidable dealings with difficult people, try to minimize direct, one-on-one contact with them. With more people nearby, the negative energy of difficult people will dissipate and be absorbed by others' energy, as opposed to any negativity being focused on and absorbed by *your* energy system alone.

Where you have a choice, always try to attract friends and acquaintances who are positive, sincere, and truly care about you. Being around comforting people makes for a more balanced and happy life. To help bring good people into your life, make a daily affirmation enumerating your own positive traits, such as warmth, loyalty, sincerity, and compassion. Request the same in family, friends, acquaintances, and coworkers, asking universal energy to send only good, positive people into your life. With such strong thoughts and the support of the universal consciousness that hears you loud and clear, better relationships will enter your life. As for the negative people in your life, you may see them soften up a bit.

If your contact with these difficult people is more constant because you live or work with them, you need to make interactions more than just tolerable. When you know you will be encountering a negative person, be sure to first envision them surrounded by a shield. That shield stops their energy from attaching to yours. This is a great exercise because just the thought of placing a shield in front of the difficult person weakens their hold and, of course, doesn't keep you on edge, maybe even making you laugh.

What should you do after encountering difficult people? Try the citrus spray and the sea salt shower discussed previously. Remember, none of these tools are "magic"—they are just useful things that help change or at least dissipate negative energy vibes. You may have your own method. If it is natural, effective, and harms no one, use it.

Below are my four truths about people with challenging attitudes:

1. They are here to stay.

2. They are multiplying fast.

3. They are caught in a web of negativity.

4. They are lifelong recruiters to their "misery loves company" network of other difficult people.

No matter how many strategies we use to cope with difficult attitudes, we will never escape them. They will always be part of our lives. Let us all vow to handle them properly and not get caught up in their negativity. Pray for them if you like, but most importantly, vow to never become like them. Freeing ourselves from their negative grasp keeps our energy free to open the sixth sense.

Junk Thoughts

The second type of junk is what I term "junk thoughts." Junk thoughts include any and all types of negative thinking. Junk thoughts are a waste of time and energy. To summarize junk thoughts, I've categorized them into two categories—outwardly directed and inwardly directed. Let's discuss both.

Outwardly Directed Junk Thoughts

Outward directed junk thoughts include senseless negative criticism, ill-spirited opinions, gossiping, wishing bad luck on people, and singing songs with negative lyrics. People, places, and things can all be the subjects of junk thoughts. These kinds of thoughts run so rampant today that they're almost a national pastime. Our minds have become what I call "trash cans" of compacted negative thoughts.

Although it's good to always have an opinion about things because it strengthens your character and makes you a good critical thinker, always thinking negatively is a problem. Have as many beliefs as you want, but make it a habit to find at least one good aspect about whomever or whatever you encounter.

Keep in mind that our thoughts are strong and powerful things. Once a thought comes into the mind, it enters the ethereal body and acts like an antenna that attracts like thoughts via the universal consciousness. We may not be able to physically see thoughts, but the antennae of others can immediately sense them on an ethereal energetic level. The process is similar to putting a question or comment on an Internet listserve. Someone will answer. The problem with junk thoughts is "like attracts like," and with lots of negative thinking comes an invitation for all things negative to enter your energy field and become real. Unless the negative pattern is broken, negativity snowballs and invites more of itself into your life.

The power of thoughts has been known throughout the ages. Remember when you were young and on your birthday were told to close your eyes, make a wish, and blow out the candles on your cake? Perhaps you also remember looking at the stars and wishing on a shooting star. There is much truth in such old-fashioned traditions. Making a wish and blowing out the candles, as well as wishing on a star are methods of moving thoughts out of the head (intangible) and into action (tangible). Prayer is a good example of the power of thought. When we pray, we send out a request in the form of a thought (intangible) with the hope that it will be answered in the form of an action (tangible).

Inwardly Directed Junk Thoughts–
The "Ould'ves"

An inward direction of negativity includes the well-known process of reviewing or rolling around in your head what I call the past or future "ould'ves." The "ould'ves" are "I should've," "I could've," "I would've," and "I might've." How do the "ould'ves" play out negatively in our lives? After something bad happens to us and we don't think we properly reacted in the moment, we go over and over in our heads what we should've, could've, would've, or might've done. The thinking process of the "ould'ves" works like this: "If she says this, I'll say that," "If he does this, I'll do that." Although planning how to handle people and events in the future is important, set a specific time to do so and focus on your plan of attack at that time. It does no good to spend every waking hour consciously going over the same thing again and again *ad nauseam*. There are no positive outcomes to the past or future "ould'ves"–they are a waste of time. In addition, the initial problem gets bigger and bigger and more and more complicated in your head. When the time does come for you to confront the problem, you are so confused about what the original issue was, that your statements have no impact at all or they make no sense. In addition, sometimes problems resolve themselves without any words or actions.

Spiritual Strategies to Handle Junk Thoughts

Begin right now to consciously replace every negative thought with a positive one. Keep in mind that you're not being asked to like something you don't. You are being asked to tweak your thinking to find something good in the midst of negativity. As an example, let us assume you saw a movie and your first response was "I hated everything about it." Stop right there. Dissect the movie. It may have had an infantile theme, the acting could have been terrible, but maybe one scene was beautiful, or the costumes were great. Focus on that as the positive. Now you have moved out of the realm of junk thoughts.

When a negative thought comes to mind, substitute it, for example, with the image of your favorite person's face or the image of a beautiful flower. This is actually a very difficult thing to do, but if you train yourself to do so, you'll be happier for the effort. Replacing a negative thought with a positive one will have the added benefit of creating abundance, and more and better things will come into your life. Positive thinking also gives you an increased feeling of physical and emotional well-being.

Junk Things

Junk things are any types of material clutter in whatever you consider "your space," be it your home, bedroom, cubicle at work, and/or your car. If you want to clear the mental cobwebs to help your sixth sense advance, clear your space. All your spaces should be clean, uncluttered, and organized. If something is no longer useful, get rid of it. Cleaning the junk out of your space relaxes the body and the mind. You can get more done in less time and your end results will be more accurate. When your space is clear, you spend less time looking for something and more time on the task. Removing junk from your life will allow your mind to relax and freely receive higher sense messages. The interpretation of the messages will also be more correct. Cleaning out junk is a form of unburdening, as described later in this book.

Sometimes it is difficult to spend time doing a major cleaning out. It could take weeks or months depending on how large your space is and how much junk you have accumulated. Because of the complexity of the job, I always break down every major task into its smallest parts. Clean out one drawer or one shelf or any small space in a room each day. It may only take five minutes to do each day, but at the end of the month, you'll have cleaned out thirty drawers, shelves, or small spaces!

In addition to cleaning one small space per day at both home and office, I also include gardening as part of my energetic cleaning up and clearing out. As time has passed, my cleaning job has gotten much easier because there isn't much to do. I constantly move things around for a different look and often give things away for someone else to enjoy. When I finish, I always feel more focused and grounded, but above all, I feel optimistic and hopeful for the future. My heightened senses always feel clearer and more receptive when I clear out junk things. You may notice that as an added benefit, sometimes that same night or a night later after the major clean out, you may have a very positive prophetic dream.

Do not just move junk from one place to another to think about later. Make a decision. If the item is no longer useful and/or salvageable, it should be discarded. If the item is useful for someone else, give it away. Let another person enjoy it.

For the purpose of changing energy, when you clean, remove all items from a drawer, shelf, or space and clean them and the drawer or the space itself before putting the items back. In addition, you should also paint, polish, or fix anything that is broken. If possible, wipe down the drawer or space with an organic cleaner. As an added energy benefit, when you have finished cleaning use the citrus spray mentioned in the "Freedom" chapter. Lightly spritz in rooms and around furniture to change energy vibrations and to move out negative, stagnant energy that has made its home in those spaces.

Try to avoid clutter on furniture surfaces. Put only a few items on tabletops. Don't crowd items on shelves. The more free space there is on a shelf, in a drawer, and in a room, the more energy freely circulates and is less likely to get stuck. Since our living and work spaces are extensions of ourselves, we want energy to be light and easy moving so that positive people, places, things, and experiences can freely enter our lives and not be blocked.

As for your work space, if you need to keep several items on your desk, get organizers for paper, pencils, works in progress, reading material, etc. Put everything in its proper place at the end of the day.

You will see that if you manage the junk in your life, the energy around you will change. As energy more freely circulates, energetic blockages collapse and the sixth sense heightens. Newness in all its aspects freely comes to you because you opened the door to the universal consciousness in every part of your life.

John's Lucky Clean Out

John was an excellent computer programmer but lost his job due to company downsizing. His job search became a full-time job. He spent upward of ten hours a day applying.

After months of no response, about to lose his unemployment and soon thereafter to lose his home, John did a massive cleaning up and clearing out of his house. As he was just finishing up the last of the cleaning, he got a call for a job interview and was immediately offered the position. He has since been able to modify his mortgage and keep the house. John claims once he decided to clean out the house, he literally felt like he was clearing out old, stagnant energy, and opening the door for better things to come.

Keep Journals

In order for you to progress in your higher sense development, you must keep a journal of your sixth sense experiences. Memories are short, but pens are long, so you must document all sixth sense information. The journal should be continuously studied and reviewed because it is a fluid, dynamic document composed of wisdom and guidance remaining as a point of reference for the rest of your life. The entries should contain detailed descriptions. As an added benefit, by keeping a journal you stay focused and deliberate in your sixth sense progress.

How to Keep a Journal

You can keep a journal in long hand, or on your computer. Although it may sound old-fashioned in our automated world, I prefer to hand-write my journal, but that's my personal preference. To me, writing by hand makes the journal and the process of journaling more personal and deliberate. When I write out my entries, my subconscious mind is more at work than when I am at a computer with the conscious mind taking over. At times the handwriting itself makes for easier and greater recall of what I may have forgotten, such as a deep sentiment I felt with a particular dream. If there's any downside to keeping handwritten journals, it would be their lack of searchability, which isn't an issue on a computer. If you're searching for a particular item you dreamed about but cannot remember when, the computer's search would take seconds, whereas a handwritten journal search could take hours. One remedy is to handwrite the journals but index them on the computer, giving you the best of both worlds.

My journal is my lifeline—it is my encyclopedia of sixth sense help and guidance. My journal is made up of a three-ring binder and loose leaf paper. Every year, I buy a new binder, always choosing a binder with a very bright color. I want a "happy" color to surround the documentation of what I record in the journal. At times, I choose a color similar to the color of the chakra I wish to develop or adjust over the next year.

You can keep a yearly journal for each of the senses you wish to develop, or you can keep one automated journal with several columns set up side-by-side to see the interrelationships among all the senses you are developing as an overlap of sixth sense advancement.

To help you better maintain a journal, here are some tips:

- **Be clear about your intention.** Before you even begin to write in the journal, take time to think about and decide which sense you wish to develop, how, and why. Choose also the sixth sense tool or tools you wish to aid you in your development. For example, you may choose claircognizance as your sixth sense and dreams as the tool. Next, focus on what the tool will do for you. Continuing the above example, would you want dreams to help with creativity in all aspects of your life? Would you like dreams to serve as the "double check" or the affirmation that the decisions you make in life are correct? Deciding which sixth sense to develop and which tool or tools you'll use to get there are important for advancing the higher senses and providing the foundation to your focus, direction, and purpose.

- **You must make entries in the journal constantly and consistently**. I suggest you enter something in the journal every day. If you are serious about your sixth sense development, I don't recommend skipping even one day. If there is nothing to report—if you cannot recall having a dream, for example—record it as such by writing the date and the word "nothing." If you are away on business or on vacation and decide to leave your computer or journal at home, bring enough filler paper to hold you over for the duration of the trip. Make an entry every day. When you get home, just input the data into the computer or place the pages in the journal binder. However you make up for entries away from home doesn't matter—do not skip one day of journal entry. If you do, your focus will weaken. Among the several characteristics needed to advance the sixth sense, constancy and focus are very important ones.

- **You must record every detail of every sixth sense message.** It is very important you record every sixth sense message you receive. If you use dreams as your method to develop your sixth sense, record every aspect of your dream immediately upon waking. Although the theme and the major parts of the dream are always important, the fine points may prove to be even more crucial to a dream's meaning. Particulars such as a color, the size or position of something, anyone present, an obvious focal point, or any symbols that appear are very important. If you wait until later in the day to document your dream, never assume you will remember all of its details. You will definitely miss crucial parts; therefore, upon awakening, take the time to record every detail. You'll get better and faster at detail recording as time progresses.

- **Divide the page vertically in half.** This can be done manually or on the computer so that each page will have a dual purpose. One purpose is to record the message. The other purpose is to record the message's manifestation later in time. If your dream is prophetic, you will later record next to the details of the dream, the details of its manifestation. One side of the page will include minute details of the message, the other side minute details of its manifestation. By putting the two side by side, you will see similarities and differences between the two. The similarities and differences help in monitoring and improving your sixth sense progress.

- **Be consistent with your journal recordings.**
  As mentioned previously, I recommend putting sixth sense messages on one side of the page. In addition, always use the same color ink for the details of the message, but use a different color for the details of the dream's manifestation. I always use the color black, for example, to record the contents of a dream. I always use red ink for its manifestation. By being consistent with both ink colors and page placement, I know automatically whether I am reading the details of a dream or its manifestation. This has worked for me. By being consistent, detailed, and organized in my journaling, I have found reliable patterns. The patterns in the journal become your personal mini-dictionary of symbols that you will add to and rely on for the rest of your life. I cannot emphasize enough that you must find a method that works for you. Once you do, use it consistently. As for timing from prophecy to actuality, everyone's timing is different. The journal will allow you to take notice of how far into the future you can expect events to occur, how often you receive predictions, under what circumstances, and how detailed and targeted the predictions are.

- **Review.** Take time to review the journal. Take notice of similarities and differences between sixth sense information and manifestation. Think about the symbols, colors, people, and places in your dreams. Patterns will begin to emerge. Use the journal for any sixth sense tools you employ as both a springboard to sixth sense advancement and as an assessment tool to periodically evaluate your progress.

Let's end this chapter with a prophetic dream that was journaled and later came true.

Marilyn's Excellent Journal Entry

Marilyn had a very simple dream—she was smiling while her friend Bruce handed her a box of Valentine's Day chocolates. To her, the dream was unusual because instead of the box of chocolates being the traditional red, the box was navy blue. When Marilyn woke up, she recorded the dream's details in her journal with its strange symbolism and forgot about it.

Several months later, Bruce invited Marilyn to his house for a dinner party. At the party, Marilyn met a friend of his named Dean, who was dressed in a blue suit that day. Dean's surname was "Valentine." As she shook his hand, Marilyn immediately recollected the dream.

She couldn't wait to get home to review the journal entry and all the details of that unusual dream. Marilyn knew her dream was prophetic and she also believed Dean was surely to be a new love interest that would have a major positive impact on her life. What clued her in on the love interest? The sweetness and desirability of the dream's chocolates were her hints.

As a postscript to the story, Marilyn and Dean are inseparable and are indeed a perfect match.

Why would the universal consciousness filter the information in a dream to Marilyn months before she met Dean—in other words, what purpose does it serve to have prophetic dreams like this? They happen for many reasons, some of which are to give hope to discouraged people, reassuring them that love is on its way. Another possible reason for having dreams that foretell future events may be a call to get one's life in order. In Marilyn's case, having the dream was like the universal consciousness giving her time to make preparations for her new love's appearance.

Love

The sayings, "everything begins with love" and "love never dies" are timeless. Love is the foundation of everything. Love is the source. From love everything flows, and so love is the foundation of all sixth sense experiences. Love is the reason universal wisdom and knowledge exist and are available to us all.

As you grow in your sixth sense development, your love for yourself, others, and for all of creation will grow and deepen because your chakras—the heart chakra especially—will expand. With its expansion, comes a wiser, greater, and deeper understanding of love's essence.

Because love has such a strong connection to sixth sense development, I want you to use love as a tool for your growth and development. Take some time to list and think about all the different types of love that exist in the world. Here are some examples to get you started: true love between a man and woman, the love between a parent and child, and the love of friendship.

Now think of the different types of love you feel for others and that others feel for you. How do you project love to others? Are you generous with kind words and deeds? How do you receive love in return? Are you gracious when people go out of their way to help you? Extend your thoughts of love to that which God has for you and all creation. Think about the limitless, mind boggling love extending to you from the universal consciousness. Now you have a glimpse at the power of love. As you focus your thoughts on love, you should feel an energy response in and around the heart chakra. Developing the sixth sense with proper and pure motives in a spirit of love is the only way to develop strong spirituality and oneness with the universal consciousness.

We will now leave the philosophical realm of love and focus more on love as a sixth sense development tool.

The following are two important mottoes by which to live a life of love:

1. Approach everyone and everything in life with respectful love.

2. Whosoever should cross your path and need

your help, human or nonhuman, always offer your love in the form of assistance that you can and will provide, and not what someone else pressures you to give.

Respectful Love

The love you should feel for all beings is what I refer to as respectful love. Respectful love wishes nothing short of the best for everyone and everything as they travel the journey of life. Respectful love is being thoughtful, looking outside oneself, and taking action to help others in times of need.

Of course, you don't have to like everyone or everything—you only have to feel respectful love for all beings on a large and small scale. Respectful love encompasses all entities, whether they are human, animal, or plant.

Respectful love is generally lacking in our society. We are tending toward more impolite, crass, and sarcastic. One of society's favorite pastimes is to watch television shows that negatively criticize creative types, such as singers, dancers, designers, models, and chefs. The more heartless the criticism, the more enjoyable the television show for the audience, and the higher the television show's ratings. High ratings mean that more shows of this type get produced. Why are these shows so loved?

Do we as a society feel so unhappy about our plight in life that we enjoy watching someone else squirm and feel devastated after their hopes and dreams are gone? Does watching someone being put down make us feel better about ourselves?

In addition to critical television shows, two major areas in our society where respectful love is lacking are big city school systems and the legal system. There are so many others, but I chose these two areas because almost everyone has had contact with at least one of them at some time, and I've worked in both.

In the school systems, especially in the larger cities, many students do not respect their teachers, administrators, and the school rules. The amount of school violence, especially directed against teachers is unprecedented. On the other hand, some teachers talk to and treat their students in a demeaning way. Both sides are, at times, not feeling or projecting much respectful love, just perpetrating unproductive negativity.

In the legal system, many clients treat their lawyers very poorly, especially public defenders. Lawyers are also known to treat each other very poorly. Many judges and their staff have bad attitudes and can be quite nasty and rude. I believe it will take years to repair the system. To illustrate how commonplace the poor treatment of lawyers is, the following is presented.

George's Atypical Day in Court

George had several hearings one day in front of several ill-mannered members of the bar and judiciary. His last hearing of the day was in a different courthouse across town. He arrived at the hearing, introduced himself, the client, and the case, but the judge stopped him cold. Taking George by surprise, the judge asked how he was doing and how his day was going so far. When George glanced directly at the judge, he saw a man with the most pleasant face looking at him with kindness and sincerity in his eyes. George thanked him for his very considerate inquiry and continued on with business. Wow, what a difference! George's case was heard with the respect it deserved.

George thought about the day's events. He was so grateful for civility, but then realized he was being ridiculous—respectful love should not be much to ask for in a day's work. It should already be there.

Animals

In addition to the way people treat other people, many people treat animals with no respect and no love. Many people discard animals when they are no longer "useful," such as when a pet is sick or dying, or when people become tired of it. The animal is then disposed of like yesterday's rubbish.

A known fact at vacation resorts is many parents get a cat or dog to keep the children occupied during the summer months. At the end of summer vacation, when it is time to go home, many people leave behind that same dog or cat to fend for itself in the soon-to-be approaching cold and barren fall and winter months. These people go on with their lives while the pet that was once pampered and cared for now has to find food and shelter on its own in a cold, barren, ghost town, which is an almost impossible situation with an unlikely happy ending. If the child feels sad leaving the pet behind, the parents assure the child that the pet will be fine because it is made for the outdoors, and will make friends and find lots of food on its own. On the contrary, the suffering this animal will experience is unthinkable. As you can imagine, this situation harms both the animal and the child. It is obvious the pet will suffer without a doubt in every way. Of course, in and of itself such behavior perpetuates irresponsibility and feelings of coldness toward any kind of life.

When one lacks respectful love, the heart chakra is not fully open. It is irregular in shape and becomes rigid. Only when a greater feeling of connection and respectful love is felt for all of creation can the heart chakra recover and open to the universal consciousness, thereby helping to advance the sixth sense.

Plants

In addition to the negative treatment of people and animals, many people disrespect plants. Plants are trashed when they no longer fit the look of the garden or the décor of the house. People constantly throw out hardy flowers when they wish to re-plant different flowers for a different look. Make it a habit to not discard any plant you no longer want. Either give the plant to someone who will take care of it and appreciate its beauty, or just put it in another location in your house or garden.

Plants are living entities. They have their own feelings. They respond when the environment is excessively hot, cold, dry, or wet, and when they are damaged in any way. Plants also respond with hearty growth to a human's kind touch or to the sound of beautiful music.

Aside from herbalists, horticulturists, and others who work with plants, I haven't met many people who practice respectful love toward plants. One exception was Dan. Dan clearly understood not only the place plants have in our world to beautify it and make it healthy for us every day, but also that plants are living, breathing, and feeling entities in their own right. Plants need to be cared for and have an important place in our homes and hearts. Dan is no longer with us, but he was a remarkable human being for his huge heart and innate knowledge that all life is important.

I beautify my home and office with plants, but sometimes I have too many or they may no longer look good where I placed them. Instead of discarding them, I have a table in the house and in the office just for plants that have no specific place. That table is their special place. It not only looks very pretty by itself, it also makes the room look absolutely stunning. Whatever you do, don't throw a live plant in the trash to die. Find a new place or new home for it.

Begin today by practicing respectful love toward all. You will feel an inward peace and contentment. The lucky recipients of your actions will feel your kind love and concern. On an energetic level, your heart chakra will open because you are stimulating the positive energy of love. With an open heart chakra, you will automatically help to attract all good things into your life and help develop your sixth sense.

Music

An old saying muses that the sounds of violin strings are the closest sound to the angels' voices we can perceive. When I listen to a truly masterful violin piece, I would have to agree. One can be moved to tears by the intensity of a masterfully performed violin piece, as the music penetrates and opens the solar plexus, aiding the acceleration and rhythmic movement of energy.

Music and the sixth sense are intimately interrelated. For example, music composed primarily of string instruments, such as the violin or the harp, relaxes the mind and body, working on the higher chakras to open them. String instruments relax the chatter of the psyche by producing alpha waves in the brain, thereby opening the higher sense channels. In and of itself, music does not develop the sixth sense—it helps facilitate its development. Music is a tool that when used purposefully and systematically, increases sixth sense sensitivity. The higher chakras open to a higher consciousness and sixth sense abilities soar.

Music of Choice

To use music as a tool for your sixth sense development, begin by determining what type of music and which musical instruments have a positive effect on you physically and emotionally. The impact this music has on you should be one of relaxation and an inward feeling of peacefulness. Do not choose music that makes you feel hyper or evokes any type of memory, whether happy or sad. The music you choose for sixth sense development is *your music of choice.*

Once you know your music of choice, you should reserve your listening to it for the times when you focus on higher sense development. Listening to music for sixth sense development is purposeful, like studying for an exam. If you study at a certain place, at a certain time, and you focus completely on the topic to be covered by the test, you will study it faster and retain more than if you study the topic piecemeal on the bus, during breaks at work, or while you are giving your dog a good run in the park. Do not listen to your music of choice as background music while you work or do chores. You may also want to stop listening to your music of choice for recreational purposes, at least in the beginning of your sixth sense development

Your music of choice must be used in a very purposeful and systematic way. It should be used sparingly to make its effect more intense. Whenever you use it, I suggest you listen to it as part of a sixth sense development routine. In addition, take time to use music as a sixth sense tool on and near the religious holidays. It is at this time during the year when the veil is said to be thinner and sixth sense development can accelerate. Also, always be sure when you use music as a tool, you are in no way rushed. Your mind should be as clear as possible and you should be free from interruptions, otherwise, save it for another day.

Matthew's Secret Musical Homework

Matthew, a jingle writer for television and radio commercials, has a secret. His secret is a routine he calls his "secret musical homework," which he always does prior to working on a client's project. The routine begins with Matthew sitting briefly in his "sacred place," a designated corner of his home office. As he breathes deeply and purposefully, he closes his eyes and empties his mind of all thoughts and distractions. Matthew then focuses briefly on the nature of the project he's been asked to do and what sort of result he wants. He then listens briefly to his music of choice and ends by emptying his mind. Though he consciously composes his music, Matthew is amazed at what a great job he can do in little time. He never lacks clients because his creativity is second to none.

As you work with your music of choice, you will notice how it helps the body reach a state of balance. Physical signs of harmony will be present. For example, vertebrae in the neck and back feel like they are falling into alignment, the heart rate and pulse will slow to a healthy relaxed rate, and aches and pains subside a bit. The state you reach is very conducive to opening the sixth sense for creativity to flow through. Once you reach a deep meditative state, your goal is clear. The ball is now in the universal consciousness' court to take over and give guidance.

There are some new age composers who claim that when their musical pieces are played, the highest chakra will open. Others claim that listening to any type of classical music will allow your body to relax, thus allowing sixth sense development to take place on its own. While new age music and some pieces of classical music are beautiful and much healthier to listen to than most popular music, just listening to music is not enough to develop your sixth sense. There is no musical "key" that automatically opens the door to other worlds or higher knowledge. Remember, music is a tool—you must take it with a clear intention and goal; and have a mind, body, and spirit that are open and receptive. There is no instant musical method to promote or quicken any sixth sense development—it is an individual experience and needs time, determination, and consistency to reach fulfillment.

Nourishment

The mind, body, and spirit are connected as one. As of late, we as a society have been abusing our bodies with fast food, alcohol, drugs, minimal sleep, and excess in almost every aspect of our lives. These bad choices have taken us away from nature, balance, and contentment.

This book encourages you to affirm your desire to live a healthy lifestyle and take steps necessary to stop a lifestyle of sensory depletion. This chapter focuses on nourishment of the mind, body, and spirit as a sixth sense tool.

Sixth sense development in and of itself is a form of nourishment. By heightening the senses and opening to the universal consciousness, we accept and act on the guidance, wisdom, and love made available to us just for asking. By opening up to the sixth sense, every part of our lives are nourished and improved.

If you were born with a well-developed sixth sense, but chose to live an unhealthy lifestyle, your sixth sense abilities would become weakened. Basing any type of decision on information from a weak sixth sense can be disastrous. The sixth sense is like the antenna on a television. If the antenna malfunctions, you may get part of the show's content between the interruptions. The remainder you fill in with your imagination. What you fill in could be wrong. It is the same with the sixth sense. If your intuition, for example, is no longer sharp, you may misinterpret or misread a sixth sense message because your judgment is clouded. The typical way to misread a message from the intuition, for example, is to think the gut feeling is telling you to act when it is really telling you to refrain from acting. The gut feeling is misread because you cannot feel the true positive or negative nudge. By acting on the misread message, you may be setting yourself up for a destructive decision and all its short- and long-term repercussions. The following example not only illustrates how easily this can happen, but also how often.

A Common Catastrophe

Let's say you made a life-changing decision (such as buying an expensive home) based on clouded judgment from a weak intuition. That one bad decision could have a negative domino effect on all parts of your life. To illustrate, say you decide to purchase the expensive home based on your income and that of your spouse, including overtime and bonus pay, as you couldn't afford the house on straight pay alone. One year after buying the house, you might unexpectedly lose the overtime and your spouse could get laid off. A strong intuition may have cautioned you from buying that particular house with a nudge that incomes would change shortly. Unfortunately, as things are, you wouldn't be able to afford the house, and there would be considerable disharmony in the household. You and your spouse might argue all the time over money. The children might become unhappy and their grades would suffer. You might even lose the house to foreclosure. The marriage wouldn't be able to sustain the stress and it would end, but with a bitter custody battle. Look at all the irreparable harm that snowballed from one bad decision stemming from weak intuition!

The *Wells*, *Nos* and *Dos*

To facilitate sixth sense development, you need to nourish your senses and live by the *Wells*, *Nos*, and *Dos*. The *Wells* are about eating, thinking, and sleeping *well*. By following the *Wells* you become centered, balanced, and focused.

If you want to take the *Wells* one step further, follow my list of *Nos*. A good rule of thumb is not to do or consume whatever clouds the senses. I understand it is a lot to ask, but if you really want to develop the higher senses to their capacity, you should continuously nourish the senses with nature's best so that the higher senses can do the same for you.

If you cannot completely avoid the items on the list, at least restrict their use. Here's my list of *Nos*:

- *No* alcohol use
- *No* illegal drug use
- *No* refined sugar
- *No* caffeine
- *No* excess (e.g., work, recreation, eating)
- *No* missing sleep

Moving to the other side of the continuum, let's look at the *Dos*. *Do* find balance in your life by making a promise to take time for yourself and find happiness, even if it's the smallest thing. *Do* go out into nature as much as you can. Above all, *do* follow all the advice of this book as much as you can!

We've already discussed food and its importance in sixth sense development. Let us focus on a few spiritual methods to nourish the senses.

You may wish to try various plant remedies available at most health food stores. Many large retail food stores carry them in the health food aisle. Be sure they are pure oils, as you do not want them to be mixed with any other ingredients. Plant remedies have no negative side effects; you cannot become addicted to them or overdo them. A few drops of the correct plant essence in a small glass of water or a few drops under the tongue go a long way toward relaxing and strengthening some aspects of the body, mind, and spirit, thereby opening the senses.

Beautiful aromas and certain essential oils also seem to naturally nourish the senses. By using your sense of smell as a tool, your body can freely relax, open the heart chakra, and encourage the energy field to open wider and flow more rhythmically. I find that sandalwood, lavender, rose-petal, and any citrus oil are all beautiful scents and excellent tools and facilitators to open the sensory channels. All are good, you just have to choose which of them you like or need the most. Experiencing essential oils can be as simple as putting a drop or two on a cotton ball and holding it close enough to your nose to enjoy its aroma as you breathe deeply and empty your mind.

Olfactory and Oil

Another way to experience essential oils is to sit in a quiet place and begin breathing deeply while emptying the mind of all thoughts and distractions. As you feel your body relaxing, take both hands and rub them together to create heat. At the point where your hands feel so hot sparks may fly off, take your favorite oil and put a drop on either index finger. Immediately place the drop of oil directly onto the third eye. Rub the third eye with your finger in a circular, clockwise motion for about one minute. While still relaxed and breathing deeply, place another drop of oil on the heart area. Again rub the oil in a circular, clockwise motion. Continue to breathe very deeply and feel your energy being activated. Enjoy the beautiful fragrance of the scents from the oil. Relax and focus. Feel the heart chakra open, and feel the energy around you moving rhythmically and orderly. You can stop when you are ready, but as this is a very powerful exercise, take a few minutes to relax afterward.

Sight, Hearing, Taste, Touch, Smell

On a day-to-day basis, try to nourish and fill your senses with positive stimuli as much as you can. For example, try to fill your eyes with as much visual beauty as you can. It can be the beauty of nature in a park, a body of water, a beautiful picture or plant, and real or artificial flowers in your house. When choosing paintings or photographs for the walls in your house, choose scenes full of beauty that make you feel happy and relaxed just by looking at them. A street scene full of traffic or a collage of items crashing into each other does not have the same affect on your body, mind, and spirit as the image of a beautiful flower-filled meadow. When you look at these scenes, think about what it is that makes them so beautiful and what energetic effect they have on you. In addition, extend that mindset to see the beauty in everything you encounter with your senses. Try to fill your ears with beauty by listening to soft, beautiful music. Fill your olfactory sense with the beautiful scent of vegetables cooking. Taste each and every mouthful of food that nourishes your mind, body, and spirit. Become tactile by actually *touching* leaves, flowers, branches, and trunks of trees. The more in tune you are with all the third-dimensional human senses, the more nourished you are, and the greater your potential for advancing developing of the senses.

Many people believe that the third and four[th] [dimen]sions constantly interact with each other and [have the] closest mutual relationship and communication of [all the] dimensions. The fourth dimension is a world comp[osed] of light and thought, and is a place where feelings of lov[e,] happiness, and forgiveness predominate. We should strive to be open-minded to the existence and unique characteristics of other dimensions.

Once you open your mind to accept the existence of other dimensions, much of the so-called unexplainable in your life will make perfect sense and seem much more natural to you. You will expand your perspective on life, and within your essence, integrate the realization that there's so much more to life than what can be absorbed by the three dimensional senses. As your perception broadens, so will your openness in mind, body, and spirit. Your sixth sense will develop more naturally.

Open-Mindedness

A definite prerequisite to sixth sense development is being spiritually open-minded. When you are spiritually open-minded, you are more yielding in your beliefs and more accepting of the unexplained. You open the door to an intangible flexibility in your consciousness and more readily receive guidance from the heightened senses.

The Test

Take the following test to determine how spiritually open-minded you are:

1. Are you willing to accept what is not always mainstream about unexplainable phenomena?

2. Are you open to other philosophies, thoughts,

and explanations that may have more of a basis in trust and faith, rather than in scientific explanation?

3. Are you proactive in your own soul searching to help explain the unexplainable?

If you answered "yes" to these questions, you are spiritually open-minded and should have no problem advancing your sixth sense ability to a more heightened state.

Let's back up for a moment and think about the opposite state of open-mindedness—rigidity. When you are rigid in your thinking, it means you are firm, unyielding, inflexible, and unbending. When your thinking is rigid, your energy becomes isolated within self-imposed barriers. The barriers become increasingly dense and sixth sense advancement cannot happen.

To more fully explain open-mindedness, let us take the example of the vastness of the universe and our place in it. It almost seems arrogant to believe we are the only or the highest life form anywhere. Think about how small we as humans are in comparison to the universe. In addition, think about the possibility of other life forms occupying the universe just as we are. Simply because we cannot see other worlds does not mean they do not exist. Eyesight or any of the other human senses may not be what is needed to experience these other worlds. To experience other life forms and other dimensions, you may call forth a means of sensing that which may be nonexistent, or at least undeveloped in us as humans.

Could the existence of the fourth dimension be true? Many claim to experience it on a daily basis as existing right here, right now. The fourth dimension is the energy vibration-level most like our third dimensional world. What we are familiar with here, such as people, animals, buildings, music, places of worship, and libraries, also exist there. Just like we hear that a radio station has a "sister" station in another locale, so it is with the fourth dimension. We are a part of and still connected to the "sister" dimension. The fourth dimension is believed to exist on top of our dimension, super-imposed upon it. The fourth dimension is visually experienced one foot in front of us in the third dimension and three feet above our ground. That is why depictions of saints and angels appearing to those on earth are never viewed directly in front of or on the same level as the viewer. They are always seen "up in the air" or a bit higher than ground level. In the same way, old world spiritual or religious paintings depict people portrayed in prayerful positions looking upward toward the sky, because upward is where the world is thought to be.

Peacefulness

Sometimes sixth sense development can reach a plateau—a place where you don't feel like you're advancing any further, despite sticking to a purposeful routine. The reason? It may be that you're not feeling true inward peace.

To truly develop the sixth sense for your highest good, you must feel peace in your heart. For many, a peaceful heart is a lifelong journey; for others, it is unattainable; and for a fortunate few, a state of true peacefulness is the norm.

A state of peacefulness radiates from an energetically nourished heart chakra. The heart chakra itself is vigorously strong, open, and balanced. With a well-functioning heart chakra comes a stronger connection to the universal consciousness and a more advanced sixth sense.

How to Feel Peaceful

To establish a state of peace in your heart, you need to first become centered. Being centered and being at peace are interrelated and achievable in many ways. Following in this section are some life choices over which you have control that, when incorporated into your life, will help center and bring you peace: the divine, others, food, proper sleep, hobbies, and interests. Even if you choose to incorporate only one or a few, you will still feel improvement.

Divine

Let us begin first with the divine. The more you include the divine in your life, the more at peace you become. Having the divine in your life makes you stop and give gratitude to a higher power. You become humbled in knowing there is a force greater than you. You become introspective and begin to feel at peace while opening the sixth sense channels.

Other People

The more you think outside of yourself, the more at peace you become. By focusing on the needs of others whether they are people or animals and aiding them in any way you can, you automatically harness and direct the universal flow of energy through your energy field to that of others in need. Energy flows out of you and to someone else's aid. The boomerang affect means by helping others you become more centered and more at peace with yourself. Connected to helping others are the actual thoughts you project toward others The kinder thoughts you think, the more at peace you are. If your mind is full of kind and compassionate thoughts, love is projected to others. The heart chakra opens and sixth sense development is facilitated.

Friends

The more like-minded friends you have, the more you will grow in positive thought. Like-minded friends have similar goals and lifestyles. Their support and loyalty brings you a state of inner peace. Your positive energy feeds off their positive energy. True like-minded friends who are also focusing on spiritual development act as an additional mutual encouragement and aid in achieving peacefulness all while developing the sixth sense.

Food

One of the most important choices in life are your food choices. Food choices intimately affect your physical and emotional well-being. Illustrating this concept is very easy. Think about how you feel after eating a very healthy meal. You feel a healthy kind of full. You feel energized physically and emotionally. Now, think about how you feel after eating a huge plate of ice cream and cake. You feel bloated and sleepy once the sugar rush has worn off. You may also feel a host of negative emotions, including hyperactivity, belligerence, and depression (the "sugar blues").

The topic of food pops up over and over again in this book because of its importance to our well-being and ability to thrive. Overall, the fewer extreme foods you eat (such as overly salty and sweet), the more centered you become and the more at peace you feel. Try to eliminate or at least reduce meat and refined sugar from your diet. Replace meat with fish and/or whole grains. Replace refined sugar with whole fruit. If you tried and cannot take away these extreme foods, try doing the opposite—add whole foods to your meals. Add a whole grain, fresh vegetable, and a fruit. As you get used to the healthy addition and its positive internal and external effects, you should begin to notice cravings for natural food.

Try to limit the amount of junk and restaurant food in your diet. The more you take time to prepare your own food, the more centered and peaceful you become because whoever is preparing the food puts their energy vibes in it. In other words, when you cook, your thoughts and feelings are energetically infused into the food. A stranger who prepares your food may not have your personal well-being in mind, so it makes sense to prepare as many of your own meals as you can. Try the following—when you prepare the next meal for the family, laugh, think happy thoughts, or sing the entire time during preparation. Watch the family as they eat. They may chat more at the table and laugh easier. This also works the opposite way. If you are upset and thinking negative thoughts as you cook, the food absorbs that negativity. If you are preparing food and feel less than positive, take a few minutes to leave the food preparation, change your thoughts to happier ones, and return to cooking. Thoughts absorbed into one's food are really powerful—guide yourself accordingly. Remember the following two important concepts about food and the sixth sense:

1. The happier the cook, the happier the one consuming the food.

2. With happiness comes openness, a state of peacefulness, and heightened senses.

Sleep

Let us turn now to sleep. The more proper rest you get, especially nighttime rest, the more at peace you feel because all systems are working at optimal capacity. Try to get a full eight hours of sleep, a few hours of it before midnight. When the body is properly rested, the body,

mind, and spirit become strong and grounded. In such a
state, the sixth sense channels readily open.

Hobbies and Interests

Your hobbies and interests are an extension of you because you devote your time, energy, thoughts, and money
to them. The more wholesome and positive your hobbies
and interests, the more at peace you become. The key to
peacefulness through hobbies and interests is devoting
enough time for them to have a positive impact on your
mind and body. Once the effect is felt there, the spirit
soars and your sixth sense development is facilitated.

The more you follow the A-Z methods in this book,
the more centered and at peace you will be. The sky will
be the limit for your sixth sense abilities!

Dennis's Great Life

Dennis, a successful business consultant, made a promise
to himself years ago that he would live his life similar to
the principles of this chapter. Dennis takes very good care
of himself by eating a healthy and balanced vegan diet. He
gets at least eight hours of sleep every night, gives thanks
to the divine every day, and surrounds himself with great
friends. In addition, he treats his job like a hobby. His
reward is an exceptional intuition that opened his heart to

meeting and marrying a wonderful woman. In addition, Dennis's intuition continuously alerts him to great opportunities in business. His sharp intuition makes him a masterful business consultant—along with his exceptional education in the theory and practices of business, his intuition brings to light what is not always readily evident via numbers and observations. Dennis's business solutions and suggestions have put him in a class all by himself. He never lacks clients, has an exceptional income, and never has to advertise—all his work comes from referrals. Dennis often claims he has to pinch himself because overall, his life is like a wonderful dream.

Questioning

Questioning the universal consciousness is a great sixth sense development tool and is easy and quick to do. All you need do is focus intently on a question or issue you want answered and send it out to the universal consciousness for a response. Once it's been sent, put the question or issue out of your mind. Relax and wait for the reply. Mechanically speaking, a great deal of energy is expended in questioning the universe because the thought you send out creates a major "behind the scenes" event, similar to an energetic domino effect.

Questioning the universal consciousness can be done for two different purposes. It can be used as a progress check or assessment of your sixth sense development. Questioning in this way verifies the spiritual guidance you receive as accurate or inaccurate. It is a great method to increase confidence and trust in your sixth sense abilities.

Second, questioning the universal consciousness can be used for *growth*. In this case, you mentally think of a question for which you really need the answer, similar to posing a question on an Internet search engine. You then wait for the answer to come. Questioning the universal consciousness this way not only heightens the senses, but also gives you faith and belief in your sixth sense abilities.

Questioning as a Progress Check

Questioning the universal consciousness as a progress check is a great assessment tool. It has five parts, each of which should be done in order.

1. Think of a neutral, unemotional, nonpersonal, and noninvasive question about something or someone that has a verifiable answer.

2. Send the question out from your mind and do not think about it again (for example, "Does my co-worker, Beatrice own a pair of bright yellow shoes?")

3. Wait for the answer. Once you have the answer, move on to step four.

4. Verify the answer (for example, ask Beatrice

if she owns a pair of bright yellow shoes. Her reply may be the following, "Yes, how did you know that?" or "Yes, but I've never worn them to work.").

5. Journal the results.

There is one important rule you must follow in this exercise—never ask a question whose inquiry or answer would in be invasive, offensive, or embarrassing to anyone in any way. Such questions are off limits. Try only to ask questions that are not common knowledge, but are within the realm of appropriate topics. For example, let us assume you met a new friend, Ed. You may send out the question:

"Did Ed ever collect anything as a teenager?"

The return answer could surprise you and be quite unusual. For example, the answer in words or symbols could be "German coins and stamps." You can verify the information by simply asking Ed what he liked to collect when he was young. The information you receive is not personal, invasive, offensive, or embarrassing, but it is one that is so unusual you never could have thought it up—it had to come through the universal consciousness.

Not only is questioning the universal consciousness a great sixth sense advancement tool, it's a great incentive to help you work even harder on your development. I liken questioning the universal consciousness to a mental aerobic exercise with the return answer as an almost energetic boomerang. Try it, you'll like it! Keep practicing. If you make it part of your routine, your abilities will advance quickly. The only downside to questioning as a progress check is becoming very mentally exhausted by questioning too much. Avoid the fatigue by not overdoing.

Questioning for Growth

The second way to question the universal consciousness is to ask for specific help, guidance, or support. The purpose of this question is for personal growth and it is done very similar to the way you ask a question on the Internet search engines.

Decide specifically what you need in the form of help, guidance, or support. Mentally ask the question and wait for an answer to arrive via your senses. I suggest your question be one that keeps you on a spiritual path and helps with a problem you're having. Requests for guidance and help with family problems, health concerns, career paths, or financial alternatives are all good ones. Topics inappropriate for questioning the universal consciousness for growth are whether your neighbor is cheating on his wife, your friend's yearly salary, and so on.

Here are a few helpful parameters in questioning the universal consciousness for growth:

- Understand that you are asking a question whose answer is very important to you; as such, the subject and its asking must be concise and unemotional. Even though you're addressing the all-knowing universal consciousness, if you aren't specific in your request, unhelpful guidance or even the wrong answer may come through.
- Before making your request, ponder whether the answer to the question is for yours or someone else's highest spiritual good or not. If it is, ask it. If not, don't ask.
- Don't get discouraged if the answer doesn't come back immediately. Remain open-minded and have faith.
- Feel gratitude for the vast amount of spiritual help available to you just for the asking. Allow yourself to experience that gratitude in every part of your being.

"Hold On, Phyllis is On Her Way!"

The expression "When it rains, it pours" perfectly describes how many people feel when tragedy strikes in their lives. Sometimes after a close loved one dies, a string of hard times follow. Old anecdotal wisdom claims that the bad events that happen after the loss of a loved one are there to take our minds off the loss, allowing the dead to move on with their spiritual journey.

Whatever the reason, I can personally attest that my mother's death was the beginning of a considerable number of personal losses, including a major temporary downturn in business due to an uncontrollable event—a major change in federal laws. For a time, very little business came in and the situation became discouraging. In the evening, I spent quiet time questioning for a sign of change that hopefully was soon to come. The response of "hold on" strongly came to me, and for good reason. Phyllis, a middle aged woman, was the spark to ignite the major comeback and the reason for "holding on." She came to my office for debt problems. From the information she provided me, filing bankruptcy would not be in her best interest. I gave Phyllis suggestions on how to handle her debt problems and she was very happy with my advice. In the weeks that followed, Phyllis was the business catalyst for a huge number of referrals that continue to this day.

Unexpected Benefits

As your senses open and you practice questioning for verification and growth, not only will your sixth sense develop and your confidence in your abilities soar, you will experience more and greater sixth sense overlap, where more than one sixth sense develops without any effort. The most common overlap is with claircognizance. You will automatically know or receive unsolicited information about people, places, and things. Just understand that as your senses become more and more open, unsolicited claircognizant information may become the norm and a sure sign that your sixth sense is rapidly developing.

Overall, questioning the universal consciousness is a great spiritual exercise. It is enjoyable to do and helpful for quickly developing the sixth sense in a very short period of time. Whether you question as a progress check or for verification, you are in charge. Your free will gets activated by putting you in control of whether to accept or reject the help, support, and guidance presented. No matter what you do with the information you receive, always feel a sense of gratitude, contentment, and security for knowing there is so much spiritual help available just for the asking.

Relaxation

The word "relaxation" is quite an emotionally charged word—today everyone needs it, wants it, and craves it, but no one seems to be getting enough of it. Our lifestyles have become so busy that the well-being that results from relaxation is often put on hold.

Take control of your relaxation now and follow this chapter's guidelines. Relaxation is presented here holistically to keep you healthy and help you efficiently and effectively develop your sixth sense.

I've noticed that as we make more and more societal advances, we move further and further away from inward relaxation and harmony, and more toward sickness and discontent. Our energy flow becomes chaotic and weak because we function to the dictates of caffeine and the clock. A lifestyle like this promotes neither health nor sixth sense development.

Relaxation Defined

For our purposes, relaxation is not napping, sleeping late, or bumming around. Relaxation is a harmonization and balancing of the mind, body, and spirit. When these three elements are relaxed they are at peak performance, and you will be free to enjoy all that life and the sixth sense have to offer.

Remember:

> The more relaxed the mind, body, and spirit, the more quickly, efficiently, and effectively the sixth sense will develop.

If the mind, body, and spirit are out of balance, energy cannot circulate properly in and around the physical and ethereal bodies. All systems function at less than capacity and begin to show symptoms of dysfunction. The body experiences aches, pains, fatigue, and discomforts that may eventually become serious medical conditions. The emotions become unbalanced and depression or disordered eating may follow. The spirit is in a state of general disconnection or lack of grounding when all systems are out of sync. Sixth sense development and its resultant helpful guidance are lost. Spiritual guidance that does get through may be weak with clouded meaning.

If you add your own incorrect meaning to a weak, unclear sixth sense message or if you receive no warnings or messages at all, you are not experiencing relaxation or harmony of any kind. So what do you do it fix it?

In order to systematically relax the mind, body, and spirit, try to incorporate the following things into your life, in your own time, and in your own way. Loosen the body by loosening the mind—eat well, exercise, and get bodywork done.

The A-Z tools naturally loosen mental rigidity, having an immediate and profound relaxing effect on the body itself, aiding greatly in sixth sense development.

Eat well. Just for starters, try to eat as close to a vegan diet as you can. The life-promoting benefits of grains, vegetables, beans, and fruits are infinite. In addition, their various colors, shapes, and textures are works of art. Not only do they smell and taste great, they look beautiful too. By contrast, hamburgers, french fries, chocolate bars, and soda do nothing for health and auric beauty. Since you are what you eat, if you eat beauty you will be beautiful in every way. So eat a variety of fruits and vegetables to help promote sixth sense development. If you are still not convinced about the real benefits of eating whole foods, you may want to try this exercise—open a package of fresh meat and experience it through the senses. Look at its gray color, feel its tight texture, savor its dead smell. Next to the meat, place a plate full of colorful fresh vegetables and fruit—any will do. The visual, tactile, and olfactory contrasts you experience between the two extreme food groups will be astounding. In addition to the olfactory differences between the pungent dead flesh and the fragrant vegetables and fruits, the vegetables and fruits are alive, and therefore, made up of live cells. You should also feel through clairsentience the "aliveness" of the cells in the vegetables and fruit, and experience the dead vibe of the animal proteins.

Next is exercise, which is critical for keeping the mind-body-spirit connection working at its peak. You don't have to have a gym routine to fulfill your daily exercise. A short walk you can fit into your schedule anytime is perfect. A daily routine of stretching is also excellent exercise. Doing housework on a regular basis is great exercise because it requires stretching, lifting, pushing, pulling, and carrying. Even better than performing housework, is doing the gardening. In addition to the physical benefits of gardening, the sensory benefits of being with nature and rigorously breathing in fresh air are even more helpful in developing the sixth sense. Try also to participate in a sport you enjoy and can routinely do—you'll see that exercise can be fun.

At work, walk as much and as far as you can, beginning from the time you arrive in your car or by public transportation. Don't wait for your lunch or break time to get out of your chair. Get up from your work station as much as you can. By continuously getting up and down, you are exercising the entire body. Even the mind works better by exercising the body, adding flexibility to your thinking. Keep in mind, flexible muscles help open the chakras. Since the mind-body-spirit connection is a holistic one, a healthier lifestyle will ensure that chakras function at peak capacity, and thus, rhythmic energy will flow and sixth sense abilities will advance.

Adding bodywork to your health routine is very important. Chi energy healing, shiatsu massages, acupuncture, acupressure, foot reflexology, reiki, chiropractic adjustments, and/or any other natural holistic method you believe in will help loosen tight muscles and keep the body (and ultimately, the mind) in balance.

Be sure to tell your holistic health care professional you are following a plan to heighten your senses. They will help you keep your body flexible and do what their profession believes will help open spiritual channels. In addition, whenever you receive a holistic adjustment, take time afterward to focus on the chakras, especially the largest energy center, the solar plexus. Get in touch with how the chakras feel and how your body feels when it is in alignment. Feel the physical and emotional contentment that being in balance gives to you. Be grateful for your renewed sense of well-being.

Chester's Choice Changes

Years ago, Chester sarcastically referred to himself as a "health nut," a name that couldn't be further from the truth and one that created howls of laughter any time he and his buddies got together. The truth was, Chester was in very bad shape physically, emotionally, and spiritually. He ate nothing that could be considered a wholesome food, never exercised, and rarely did much of anything that would improve his life. Chester often joked that his only exercise was lifting his spoon. He ridiculed those in good physical shape and claimed to be the nation's #1 hater of exercise. He claimed to have an incurable "gasoline butt" and there was nothing anyone could do to help him. As time went on, it became evident that Chester was laughing on the outside and crying on the inside.

About five years ago, Chester began to evaluate his life. He didn't want to live like he had any longer—he wanted to go back to feeling more confident, as he did when he was a child. He wanted better things for himself, like a happy and more fulfilling life. Chester remembered being very intuitive as a child, but believes he lost his intuitive abilities when he began grade school. He remembered how helpful his intuition was and often referred to it as "his best friend inside."

Chester decided to get back his "best friend" and change his life by taking small but deliberate steps. He started with real exercise, not spoon lifting. He began to take care of his apartment and learned how to fix things that were broken. He began to eat right, sleep more, and center himself emotionally. He took pride in his appearance. His whole regime became a body, mind, and spirit relaxation theme. From there, changes took place and good things blossomed. Chester started to notice that his "best friend inside him" returned. Chester called on that best friend often to help in decision making. The positive changes to Chester's life snowballed. He met the woman of his dreams and landed his perfect job. His friends aren't laughing now. They're cheering his return to life— and what a great life he has!

Remember, through total mind, body, and spirit relaxation, all is connected, all will become balanced, and sixth sense development will be enhanced.

Stones

Stones, rocks, and rock formations share a unique sacredness and mystical connection to the universe and to the divine in their own quiet way. Their transformation through the ages has locked within them the wisdom and knowledge of the ages. Whether a stone is large or small, a chip or a huge formation, stones are connected to one another and to the divine. Stones, rocks, and rock formations become another tool in the sixth sense development tool box when we understand and respect their place in higher sense development.

As you read this chapter, keep in mind that each stone has its own unique properties. Determine your favorite stone, which I will refer to as your "stone of choice."

Work with it often by keeping it near you, carrying it with you, and/or wearing it.

Stones of Choice

If you have trouble determining what your stones of choice might be, think of your favorite color. What color are you always drawn to? What is your favorite color for clothing? Stop by a crystal or mineral store and hold a stone of that color in your hand. Focus on its energy vibration. How does it feel? Does it feel like it has its own positive energetic quality? Does it feel like something you would like to have in your home or office, maybe as a paperweight to keep close by while you do creative activities? Would you feel good wearing it as jewelry? Can you clairsentiently feel the stone's innate life force? As you hold it, do you feel any cranial pressure or any changes in the chakras? As you become more energetically sensitive, you will be able to feel the unique, subtle energy of each and every stone and the differences among them.

When choosing your stone of choice, you do not have to choose only one. You may choose as many as you like, but keep in mind the more stones you choose, the more scattered will be your mineral devoted energies. For that reason, I believe one or a few are all you need as a tool for sixth sense development.

The Energy of Stones

Once you have chosen your stone of choice, you should cleanse it before you work with it. One way to cleanse it is to place it in a glass of warm water and a teaspoon of sea salt overnight. The salt will cleanse the stone. As you work with stones, you will intuitively be able to determine if they may need sunlight for a few days or a charge from the earth in addition to the salt. If the stone needs earth's charge, bury it completely for a few days. Just remember where you buried it so you aren't digging up everything to find it!

Now that the stone is cleansed, you need to program it. All you do is while holding the stone in your hand mentally project what you want the stone to facilitate—for example, help balance the heart chakra, help with lucid dreaming, or help with creativity. The stone is now programmed. Keep it nearby to feel its special energy.

Let's now focus briefly on three specific stones, lapis lazuli, amethyst, and quartz crystal.

Lapis Lazuli

Lapis lazuli is a highly spiritual energized stone. Lapis lazuli not only works on opening up the chakras, especially the sixth and seventh, it also has a balancing or grounding effect on the person who is wearing it. It is an energetically strong stone and one I recommend to keep in the home, at the workplace, and/or to be worn as jewelry. This is one stone you will want to keep nearby.

Amethyst

In addition to lapis lazuli, I have found amethyst to be another great sixth sense tool. Amethyst helps to facilitate inspiration and creativity. If you wear amethyst when doing creative work you will definitely feel like you have a helping hand. When I wear amethyst, I have less episodes of writer's block.

Quartz Crystal

Quartz crystal is another widely used and excellent sixth sense tool. A clear quartz crystal placed anywhere in the house or workplace acts as a conduit of energy. Any size crystal will do the job. Some people believe the larger the crystal, the greater will be its frequency. Size does not necessarily matter when it comes to crystals; in fact smaller ones are sometimes more powerful.

Crystals make excellent accompaniments to your other sixth sense tools. Taking time periodically in a mineral store to sensitize yourself to the various stones and energies is in itself a great sixth sense development tool. You are never too young to appreciate the spiritual value of stones, as the following story of the "stone intuit" will tell.

The Stone Intuit

Years ago, I had a client who I'll call "Grandma." Grandma needed to see me immediately for an emergency legal issue. She was torn about what to do, because although she needed to see me right away, she was babysitting her granddaughter, Precious. Grandma had no one with whom to leave Precious while she came to my law office. I told Grandma to bring Precious with her, and my secretary would be happy to watch her in the reception area while we discussed business.

Precious was about six years old, and couldn't contain herself while Grandma and I exchanged pleasantries before our meeting. When we had a break in the conversation, Precious asked if she could show me her special collection of stones. As she opened her little purse and took each one out one at a time, she told me the stones "spoke" to her in their own special way. She loved each one of them, and she kept them with her all the time. She told me they went through so much and had so much to teach us. Precious gave each one of the stones a special name to go with an individual personality. It was a beautiful experience to watch this highly developed and highly sensitive child talk divinely about the uniqueness of stones. There was an unbelievable maturity and deep wisdom within her. She was truly an advanced soul among much less advanced souls. While Precious was telling me about her love for her stone collection, her grandmother looked at me and embarrassedly rolled her eyes as if to say "what nonsense."

I sometimes think about Precious and Grandma. I think about how sensitive and special this little girl is. Her abilities should be encouraged and developed, and not mocked. It seemed that Grandma didn't know the honor bestowed upon her—she was the grandmother of a highly advanced intuit. I hope others do not stifle Precious's dear gift and beautiful sensitivity.

Please incorporate stones as a tool in your sixth sense development. Their strong energy vibe will work along with your energy to help open the chakras and let in the universal energy to facilitate more sixth sense experiences.

Trust

How do you know what you perceive through your well-developed higher senses is real and not simply your thoughts or imagination playing tricks on you? How do you know that what your intuition is telling you is accurate and should be trusted?

Confidence = Trust

You must mentally get to the place where you just *know* the messages, nudges, and feelings you receive through the sixth sense are real. You do this in your own way and in your own time. But to get you there faster, remember this about the progression of sixth sense development: As you continuously practice becoming more aware, your intention deepens, your internal focus becomes clear, the accuracy of messages you receive becomes very high, and your confidence will naturally follow.

As your confidence soars, so does your trust in what you perceive is true. Do not ever doubt yourself even slightly. If you do, your development will reach a plateau and not move further. You may make mistakes. Everyone does. That's why practice is so important. Don't let the mistakes in sixth sense message interpretation take away your trust and confidence. Determine how you made the mistake, put it behind you, and move on. Dissecting how a mistake was made may facilitate your sixth sense practice, but it does no good to beat yourself up over it.

To illustrate trusting in yourself and your senses, I will use the sense of hearing for our example.

Clairaudient Example

Auditory messages coming from the universal consciousness are on a higher frequency than ours and are sent more quickly than our reality's normal sound waves. If you wish to develop your clairaudient abilities, I suggest you begin by asking the universal consciousness for messages that are loud and clear enough to be heard. If you do not state this request, clairaudient messages will sound like chatter, babbling, or otherwise indistinct. They may also sound like the noise at a party where several conversations are going on at the same time, but nothing may seem to make sense. The messages have to be transmitted more slowly and clearly—if you can't hear anything, you'll become discouraged. When you finally hear a clear word, the sound itself may be shocking and you may inadvertently cut off communication. Don't worry—communication will be restored. Almost everyone at one time or another in their life has heard their name called upon rising in the morning. If it happened to you, do you remember how startled you felt not only to hear your name, but to hear your name from a voice you just knew came from beyond the veil? If it happens, take a deep breath and remain open. It will come again. Your sixth sense development will not stop. As you continue practicing, the words will return more strongly and clearly.

Is This Real Sixth Sense Communication or My Thoughts?

How do you trust what you are hearing is a directed message and not your own thoughts? Look to your pattern of speech and the sound of your thoughts.

You are familiar with your own speech pattern and the words and phrases you use when you think. Normally, your thought process is complete, that is, you don't normally think in fragments or phrases, but completed thought patterns. On the contrary, if you are given information by clairaudience, you may hear an almost inaudible sound or a partial word or phrase that needs interpretation or needs to be pieced together to make sense. The voice may have a distinct male or female sound or it could sound asexual—neither male nor female. The sound could be piercing and direct.

Pay very close attention to every word and phrase you receive. The few words conveyed are extremely pointed. Clairaudient messages never contain useless chatter. After the communication has ended and you have journaled what you received, think about the messages and what they mean to your life. Review the journal entries often, and most of all, trust in yourself and the communication.

Unburdening

Unburdening is a powerful tool for sixth sense development because it allows your mind, body, and spirit to open and experience prosperity and fullness in every aspect of your life. The act of unburdening is one of the greatest ways to manifest abundance.

Unburdening Defined

Unburdening, for our purposes, is very specific. It means clearing the conscious mind of all thoughts and distractions. As a sixth sense development tool, once a person has achieved a proper state of unburden, the mind is unbounded. The door to limitless universal guidance, wisdom, and love is wide open.

A state of purposeful unburdening is a highly elevated spiritual state of being. Unburdening is a condition of human spiritual vulnerability that reflects our spiritual sincerity and human openness to all that is positive and available for our highest good. Unburdening is an excellent tool for sixth sense development. To illustrate how important unburdening is for our sixth sense development, we will look at a thought-filled and distraction-filled mind, and then move to a discussion of a clear, unburdened mind. You'll notice the difference in energetic quality of the two states of being.

Thought-Filled and Distraction-Filled Mind

When the mind is full of thoughts and distractions, every thought leads to another thought or action. The mind directs the body and the body responds like a human robot. The body becomes the servant of the mind's wishes and commands.

A thought-filled and distraction-filled mind can last a lifetime, and in most cases, it does. As with any habit or routine, the human robot gets used to living like this from one day to the next. Days become weeks, which become months—you get the idea. Before you know it, a lifetime has passed and you have given up a great gift totally at your disposal—the universal consciousness just waiting for you to tap into it, but you never did. You were too busy thinking wasted thoughts. Instead of creating abundance, your energy flowed similar to that of a dog's when chasing its own tail. Such an activity brings no constructive result.

A thought-filled and distraction-filled mind acts like a plug, blocking sixth sense messages from getting through. Although living in our world requires thinking and acting on thoughts, plans, and ideas, you also need to spiritually recharge. When you spiritually recharge, you stop controlling the conscious mind and allow the higher consciousness to become unbounded and to operate solely on its own. When the mind is unburdened, it makes room for a whole new world of wisdom and guidance.

An Unburdened Mind

I always say an unburdened mind is easily described, but difficult to master. An unburdened mind is one devoid of distractions. Unburdening your mind of all distractions intentionally focuses your attention on whatever you're doing, whether the task is mental or physical. Being unburdened is a state of true meditation, the way it was intended to be experienced.

Whatever you are doing, be it writing a report or painting a wall, you will automatically open the higher senses to universal knowledge by intentionally unburdening or emptying your mind. Instances of blocks in creativity will lessen. If you need an answer to a problem, clearly formulate the problem in your mind and then unburden it. The answer (or at least a clue) should come to you at a later time without effort.

When you are truly unburdened, if extraneous thoughts begin to enter your mind, it's because you are not fully paying attention to what you are doing. Stop these thoughts by redirecting your focus back on the task. The key to unburdening is to direct all attention to the mechanics of the present task. If your mind is really unburdened, you're doing nothing else but the present activity. You are becoming one with the activity. At that point, the higher senses take over, opening you to the universal consciousness and allowing in guidance, love, and wisdom.

As you can imagine, multi-tasking has no place in unburdening. You shouldn't eat, drink, chew gum, talk, text, or do anything else unless it's part of the activity. You should not carry on a conversation with anyone while focusing on your task, unless it is part of the task. You should not play any kind of background music while doing a task, because music is a distraction. Background music actually encourages thoughts and distractions completely unrelated to your physical or mental task.

Unburdening Test #1

The easiest test of your ability to unburden or empty your mind is driving a vehicle. The next time you get into your car begin the unburdening thought process by focusing all attention on the driving. Do not turn on the radio or the CD player. Do not use your cell phone, and don't text anyone. Do not think of anything but the road and the traffic. Optimistically speaking, you will probably lose your focus just seconds after you turn on the ignition. You aren't alone. When most people begin to practice unburdening the mind, they can't sustain their focus for more than a few minutes. Just keep trying and you will get better at it.

Unburdening Test #2

Now try this exercise. Use this chapter as an unburdening test. Read it from beginning to end with full interest in each and every word, sentence, and paragraph. If your mind wanders, begin the chapter again. Do this until you have reached the end of the chapter without your mind wandering or thoughts popping up. Don't get discouraged—applying the concept of unburdening is one of the most difficult things you'll ever do. Just keep practicing. Everyone has to break the habit of doing and thinking of more than one thing at a time especially since our society promotes multi-tasking. As you practice unburdening the mind more often and experience all of its intrinsic and extrinsic benefits, it will come to you more naturally.

Additional Advantages to Unburdening

In addition to developing the higher senses, positive and practical by-products await when you unburden the mind. Your focus on any present task will make you more accurate and deliberate in all you do. If you are performing a more routine activity, such as data entry or even cleaning a room, your accuracy rate should be nothing less than 100 percent. Your concentration will be sharper and will last longer. As an added benefit, anything you do will take less time because you aren't slowing yourself down with daydreaming, taking needless breaks, checking and re-checking your work, or re-doing what you may already have done. You will feel more rested and not as rushed. If you tend to be a little high-strung, everyone will notice a change in you—practicing unburdening will help calm you.

If you apply unburdening the mind to what you've read, your reading speed and comprehension will rise. If you are a student, time devoted to studies will drop substantially from what you spend now. Once you master emptying the mind, your confidence will soar because you'll know everything you do is the best you can do.

Most importantly, since tasks will be completed faster, you'll have more time for fun!

In addition to the everyday practical benefits of practicing unburdening, if you are experiencing loss of any kind, focusing all your attention on what you are doing helps divert attention from your feelings of grief, helplessness, and hopelessness—even for a little while. You will build up physical and emotional strength, which aids in the healing process.

Whenever you practice unburdening the mind, you are truly in a "Zen moment." You will feel the positive effects on your body because emptying the mind is the closest activity to complete rest. The body feels stronger and more relaxed when the mind is unburdened. Overall, your stamina will increase. As a tool used in sixth sense development, unburdening helps create an empowering life, having profound effects on all parts of your existence.

Visualization

Visualization is the process of focusing on a positive mental image for a specific desired outcome. For purposes of developing the sixth sense, visualization, also referred to as imagery, is made up of a two parts that cannot exist without each other—relaxation and openness. To properly use visualization as a sixth sense development tool, you must start by being relaxed mentally, physically, and spiritually. For tips on achieving the required state of relaxation, see its chapter, the letter R. Once relaxed, a state of openness will occur to allow the senses to unlock and absorb the universal consciousness and all its benefits.

Never underestimate the power of the universal consciousness—it works in mysterious ways. Although nothing is guaranteed in this life, you have nothing to lose by employing visualization. As a sixth sense tool, visualization helps channel universal energy directly to you and (hopefully) to the result you want. Visualization, like praying for a miracle, may not always give the wished-for result, but it can't hurt and is certainly worth the effort.

A Short Exercise in Visualization

The following method of visualization is a quick, easy, and highly effective tool for sixth sense development.

1. Choose a quiet place where you can sit and be free of outside distractions.

2. Empty the mind of all thoughts and be free of internal distractions.

3. Breathe deeply. As you slowly inhale and exhale, feel your body fill with life giving oxygen.

4. Feel your body become more relaxed and more centered each time you inhale and exhale.

5. Continue to breathe slowly and deeply, but now visualize your entire being is being bombarded in an orderly fashion from every direction with bright lavender rays of light from the cosmos. The bright lavender rays of light are coming from above and below you, penetrating every part of your mind, body, and spirit. The flow

of energy is orderly, but highly charged with the universe's infinite positive energy.

6. Once you feel your mind, body, and spirit sufficiently soaked with lavender light, visualize the light moving away from you and returning to the cosmos.

7. You should feel your entire being fill with light accompanied by a feeling of calmness and contentment.

8. Continue the deep breathing, but now visualize a beam of pure gold light pouring into the top of your head through the crown chakra infusing you with knowledge, wisdom, and love.

9. Give thanks to the universal consciousness for its infinite knowledge, love, and wisdom. You are now ready to end the visualization. When you complete the visualization, take a few minutes to assess how you feel. Optimally, you should feel a residual spiritually heightened sense of being surrounded by light.

You may want to make a routine of doing the above visualization as a morning habit upon waking. It's a great way to start the day because it not only puts your mind, body, and spirit in a healthy place, it also adjusts your energy field, helps you to be alert, and acts as a proactive defense to the anticipated stresses of the day. You may also wish to do this visualization if you need help in solving a problem. This exercise takes your mind off the immediate problem, opening you to the guidance of the universal consciousness.

Following are some examples of using visualization as a sixth sense tool. Keep in mind two important points of visualization: the desired outcome should be made very clear from the beginning; and secondly, other senses may overlap and help facilitate the desired outcome.

Example 1: "The Shift"

If you're ever a defendant in a criminal matter, the best result of a case is for all charges to be dismissed. Life returns to normal and all punishments, including fines, jail terms, and charges are gone. What if you're a criminal defendant? Along with seeking proper legal advice and counsel, you can visualize the court signing an order dismissing all charges at every opportunity. If you're focused and diligent, adding visualization could open the door for events to occur that could cause delays on either side that work out for your benefit. Plausible favorable events that could occur include the opposing side not appearing in court for hearings or missing crucial deadlines, opening the door to a dismissal of the case.

Personally, after doing visualizations, I've noticed strange surprises that resulted in exactly the outcome I wanted. In the case of one client, Chris, I knew I had a big problem facing us at our court hearing. Chris was fully informed of the multiple problems facing him, but there was not much we could do; things were really tough. We had nothing left but to visualize Chris and me smiling and cheering because we won.

After several episodes of visualization, my intuition clearly told me all would work out in Chris's favor. I didn't doubt myself. The case's facts made it difficult for me to imagine how our court appearance could work out for the better, but I was happy to receive a favorable message. A sixth sense auditory message came through loud and clear—there would be a "shift." I didn't know what a "shift" meant, but I knew it would be good. On the day of the hearing, the first person to be called was not completely ready, so my case was called instead. The timing was perfect for us. It was the timing that facilitated the "shift." In the middle of presenting Chris's side of the case, the hearing officer was interrupted by his staff for a matter needing immediate attention. When he returned to us to continue the hearing, he was so distracted that he didn't continue pursuing the issue that would have adversely affected Chris. The hearing officer could have adjourned the hearing for another day, but he didn't. The outcome was favorable for us. Chris and I walked out stunned but exhilarated.

Example 2: "Stay Seated, You're Next."

As I was walking into Jay's court hearing, Jay presented me with facts that would have very adversely affected his case. There was no "wiggle room" on this one—we had no defense. All I could do was hope for the best and do a visualization of us as winners, cheering on the way out of court.

For some strange reason, traffic was almost nonexistent the day of the hearing, so both Jay and I arrived very early. Jay was very nervous and wanted to use the rest room and get a cup of coffee to pass the time. We both knew we had a long wait ahead of us, so killing some time seemed like a good idea. Just as Jay was getting up from the chair, I received a message loud and clear, "Stay seated, you're next." The message seemed incorrect, as it was too early to be called, but the message was 100 percent correct—we were called up early and at the exact moment that the problematic issue was to be discussed, the hearing officer received a call from his young son. The hearing officer was so agitated when he came back to us, that he thought he had completed his inquiry. He said he was satisfied with everything and ended the hearing. (Apparently, he needed to leave to settle his problem at home.) It turned out to be a great outcome for Jay and of course for me. Again, my client and I were stunned but exhilarated.

Try to practice visualization as much as you can. If you give it the proper time and focus, you should feel a sense of peace both during and after doing it. Try to invent your own version of visualization. The methods to do it are infinite—you'll find your own perfect way. Remember, you must practice visualization frequently for its sixth sense development effects to be realized.

White Light

As an added tool in your sixth sense development kit, you may wish to employ the power of divine white light. The divine white light, when used for sixth sense development, aids in bringing and keeping good things in your life.

How to Use the White Light

To use the powerful white light, try to find a quiet place free of distractions. Empty your mind of all thoughts and distractions, and breathe deeply. Next, mentally surround your entire being—physical, mental, and spiritual—with a clear, pure, protective, beautiful, and divine white light. Imagine that no negative energy can penetrate the protective white light. Keep this image of yourself as long as you can. As you continue to see yourself surrounded by the white protective divine light, breathe deeper and deeper. As you continue to breathe deeper, the chakras will become more open to the universal consciousness.

Benefits

When you surround yourself in the white light, you are forming a higher sense protection or a natural higher sense repellent against negativity entering your energy field. White light has a calming or centering effect on your thoughts by helping to prevent you from getting entangled in life's minutiae. The white light helps to dissipate negativity that has made its way into your life. You will become sensitive to the special energetic feelings of the white light.

I want you to try to incorporate encompassing the white light scanning exercise into your routine because it only takes a minute to do. As you mentally work with the white light over time, I want you to expand its application by doing the "scanning exercise."

Advanced White Light Application: Scanning Exercise

The scanning exercise takes the white light exercise one step further. Begin with closing your eyes, breathing deeply, and emptying the mind of all thoughts and distractions. As you breathe deeper and deeper, surround yourself completely with the white light. Next, energetically scan your entire body, starting at the top of the head, down to your feet. Every part of your body should feel energetically smooth with no blockages in or around you. If you feel a blockage, stop and focus on it. Focus on where you feel it and what it may mean. A blockage could be a warning of a problem that has not yet manifested on the physical level, giving you time to nip it in the bud. The blockage could be anything related to you, such as a problem with your health, family, work, finances, or home.

You can also surround loved ones, including family, friends, acquaintances, and pets, in their own white light "bubbles." In addition, you may also want to surround your residence, car, and place of employment in the protective white light. Try to do this every morning. All you need for it to work is a moment of focus and a slightly higher elevation of consciousness.

The following example shows how effective the white light scan is. The most important thing to take away is to use the information presented to make changes if a warning makes itself known.

Karen Ignored the Scan

Karen surrounds herself, each member of her family, and her home with white light every day before she leaves for work. For one particular week, as she watched the white light bathe all parts of her home, her mental scan always stopped at a bedroom window on the second floor, and in the right-side corner of the house. Karen thought the blockage was strange, but she is a busy person, and didn't take the time to try to understand the blockage's meaning.

Karen never did anything to divert the negative energy. Unfortunately, the warning became reality—the room where the white light stopped became the entry point for burglars who ransacked the house while everyone was either at work or school. Although Karen was born with a highly developed sixth sense, she is always in a hurry. If she had taken the time to determine the warning's meaning, she could have acted on it.

Heeding the warning could have made Karen inspect the room. Maybe her inspection would have revealed a loose fitting window that, if fixed, may have been enough to discourage thieves from breaking in.

Remember that events begin in the spiritual realm. If your sixth sense is highly tuned, you'll receive clues about what's coming. If a potential problem is brewing but is detected before it occurs, there may still be time to divert it in another direction and stop it from happening or lessen its magnitude.

Use the white light as a means of protection and sixth sense development. It can be done anytime without anyone knowing you're doing it. Just by working with the white light systematically, your sixth sense will be activated.

X-Out

Negative people, places, and things, will always be a part
of life. No amount of sixth sense development can change
the reality of their coexistence with us. Positivity and negativity are the inevitable reality of how different cosmic
forces (yin and yang) play out in our world.

As for the positive in the world, they are always welcome. Good health, true love, and lots of wealth are everyone's dream; they need no coping strategies. The more
positive people, places, and things we have in our lives,
the happier we are. Negative people, places, and things
are problematic and need to be managed.

I'd like to remind you of one very important concept
before we discuss negative people, places, and things—
we *need* the negative to teach us life's lessons. Problems,

challenges, and irritations are presented to us as tests of character, though that doesn't mean we have to be at everyone or everything's mercy. Negativity can be managed. Even negativity that is beyond your control can be managed by using various strategies.

For those of you devoted to a spiritual path who especially want a clear mind and direct focus for developing the sixth sense, I suggest you make a conscious effort to "x-out" or rid yourself of as much negativity within your control as you can. Negativity comes in all forms, shapes, and sizes. From the complainer at work and disorganized dresser drawers, to violent movies and illness and death, negativity is disguised in many ways.

Effect of Negativity on Sixth Sense Development

Remember, everything is energy—if you become entangled in negativity, your overall energy will become heavier because negativity weighs you down. Your sixth sense development will be adversely affected because you will have difficulty elevating your consciousness. The chakras will darken and close a bit. Your energy flow will become less orderly and your energy field won't be as expansive; the latter might even cave in closer to your body. The sixth sense channels become blocked, and ultimately, your sixth sense development will be stifled. The adverse consequences to your life are serious. The solution? X-out as much negativity as you can.

Strategies to X-Out Negativity

Let's begin with our strategies on dealing with negative people. You must train yourself to not get sucked into other people's problems to the point where it adversely affects your life. Consider that even a problem your child makes must be managed so it does not affect the rest of the household. You need to remain in charge—the negativity cannot take charge of you.

Although you need to help others in whatever way you can to alleviate their burdens, you cannot internalize and experience their negativity as your own. You cannot neglect your duties and responsibilities or harm yourself for someone else's mistakes. You need to remain strong, like a stone pillar, to temporarily support another's spiritual weight. You can try to help the person you're supporting find a viable solution while not adversely affecting your life and the lives of those close to you.

You can manage negativity in many ways, and sometimes the obvious answer is the most appropriate. Just say no. In the following example, Nancy illustrates what can happen to those who are taken in by others' problems, which could all have been avoided by refusing to become involved.

Nancy's Mistake

Nancy came to my office for a professional consultation on debt defense. In addition to the regret, embarrassment, anxiety, and anguish she had for her many financial mistakes, Nancy had put herself in financial jeopardy for Brian, a new love interest. Nancy gave Brian her own good credit in return for promises to pay money back as soon as Brian's personal injury settlement check arrived. The payback never came and she never heard from him again. So, Nancy sat in my office hysterically crying, feeling extremely regretful. It might have helped Nancy to realize that there's a sometimes fine line between helping someone and ruining your own life. Do not cross the line. Help others, but remain in control by not adding unnecessary negativity to your life.

Sometimes another person's negativity is extremely strong and the negative charge almost feels like it is swallowing you up. In this instance, be sure you are not feeding into the negativity. Stop it from entangling or attaching itself to you. Consciously affirm you will not allow anyone's negativity to reach or to penetrate you energy field. This is a very strong affirmation and it will help to program your psyche and energy field to not get sucked in and be affected by negative outside energy influences.

In addition, I suggest you read and re-read the chapter on junk. Incorporate into your life as many of the chapter's suggestions as you can. Also, if you are commonly in and around negativity (and who isn't?), remember to always think of yourself as surrounded in clear white light, as discussed in the previous chapter, "White Light." By following the advice in both chapters and the rest of this book, you will experience a reduction in the amount of negativity in your life. A reversal in attractions will take place. Instead of negativity being most prevalent, more positive people, things, and events will begin to make their way into your life. Your friends may sense an energetic difference about you, but not know what it is. They may ask questions like, "Did you lose weight?" "Did you get your hair done?" or "What's different about you?" You may have changed your appearance, but the real change is in your energy's charge, repelling negativity and keeping it out.

If negative people have made their way into your living or work space, change the vibe by opening as many windows in the immediate area you can. The air circulation helps to clear negative thoughts and words. Another quick fix is to spray a natural citrus room spray where the negative person was. The purity of the natural citrus air spray will change the vibes from stagnant to fresh, even if only temporarily. You can also sprinkle sea salt around where the negativity was—for example, around the chair where the negative person was sitting. Doing so helps to clear away any negative energy that may have remained.

If you believe negativity remains in a particular place, perhaps because it is frequently revisited by negative people, try the following. Cut in half a *very* fresh, shiny, large onion, preferably organic, but any kind of onion will suffice. Place both halves, cut side up, on aluminum foil on a table in the room where you experience a negativity feeling. Leave the onion there overnight. The room's energy will feel better the next day because during the night, the onion will absorb the negativity in the room. The next morning, close up the foil around the onion and discard it. Because the onion is energetically toxic, do NOT use this onion in any way—do not cook with it, do not bury it. You do not want to "nourish" your flowers or vegetables with negativity. Be sure you throw the onion in the trash or put it down the garbage disposal.

A longer term negativity repellent strategy is to make a conscious effort to live a good, balanced life in body, mind, and spirit. As discussed previously, you need to eat well, think good thoughts, say positive things, spend time with positive people, do good deeds, and focus intently on sixth sense development. Living your life in this manner automatically repels much of the negativity trying to make its way into your energy space. As you live a good, balanced life with a sixth sense development component, your strong spirit puts up an invisible barrier repelling lots of negativity without your knowing it.

What about those times negativity enters your life and you have no control over it, for example, in cases of serious sickness or injury to one's self or loved ones? The only way to x-out such negativity is to spiritually surrender to it. Surrendering does *not* mean feeling defeated or giving up hope. It is, along with doing everything humanly possible to remedy the situation, the highest form of spirit know-how. The true act of spiritual surrender raises the consciousness to such a high level that the mind, body, and spirit actually become strengthened and infused with spiritual enlightenment. The higher sense channels open, allowing in guidance to either remedy the hardship or bring peace and comfort to you during the crisis.

Try to x-out as much negativity as you can, using the methods in this chapter or as a supplement to any of your own methods. A clear mind and a reduction of negativity around you will facilitate sixth sense ability development. To keep a sense of humor when you feel yourself surrounded by negativity, think of the mantra "negativity, x-out of here." It may not always change the negative atmosphere, but it will certainly bring a smile to your face.

Yearly Assessment

You weren't born an expert. Even prodigies need direction and focus. It can take many years for you to master a particular field of study. As with any specialty, you begin with a foundation of truths and principles that are then applied to practical, real-life situations. As time goes on, you begin to notice that your knowledge base is dynamic and adaptable. Principles can and do change because unforeseen variables constantly enter the picture, resulting in the knowledge base evolving and expanding. Just as master lawyers, teachers, speakers, chefs, and writers incorporate their own personal methods in what they do, so should you with sixth sense development. Use your own creativity and background to develop your higher senses. Know that expertise depends on one's ability to remain open and incorporate newness and change. That openness is precisely how you become an expert in any area of knowledge, including sixth sense advancement.

You, the sixth sense student, begin with a background of information. The content of this book and others like it, in conjunction with your journal entries, form your knowledge base. You then apply your knowledge by practicing and getting better at perceiving and interpreting messages you receive through your higher senses. You then access your progress to determine how well you did.

You will find that at the beginning of your development process, things will feel more like an evolution than an on-and-off experience. You will notice milestones in your growth over time, and if you are truly devoted to heightening the senses, your progress will probably take no longer than a few days or weeks. My suggestion—assess improvements and changes in your abilities in large blocks of time, such as every six months or yearly.

Review versus Assessment

A review is not the same as an assessment. Reviews are mechanical and can be done daily or weekly. Performing a review would be like going through a checklist and looking objectively at how prophecy correlates to real events. For example, say you're focusing on dreams as a sixth sense tool. A review would mean looking at the content of your dreams over the last week to see which, if any, predicted what occurred during the week. A short review can take as much as thirty seconds if your whole goal is looking for the relationship of prophetic synchronicity to actual events.

On the contrary, assessment determines your sixth sense development over a set period of time. You may decide to use the end of the calendar year as the time to assess your yearly development. Begin by thinking about which sense or senses have been most heightened over the last year. Continuing the example of dreams, look at your dream interpretation accuracy, comparing content to what manifested. Calculate the time it took from having the prophetic dream, to its manifestation. You'll also look at what you learned over that period of time, for example, what symbols have what meaning. You'll look to any and all sixth sense overlap. It's from an assessment that future sixth sense goals are built.

Four Solid Results from Periodic Assessment

As time goes on, you should notice four characteristics about your assessment. Your interpretation of messages should become more precise every year. In this sense, practice does make perfect. As time goes on, you should also notice that your journal's details are becoming more refined, clear, and accurate. Third, the number of prophetic messages received should continue to increase significantly. Also take note as your confidence rises. That's right—these periodic assessments are confidence boosters. You definitely need confidence and its twin, trust, when developing your sixth sense. Doubt does much to damage your development.

When I was a professor and headed a business school, I was always focused on outcomes assessments for my students. I examined, amongst other types of information, course content, professors' teaching skills, student grades, and the number and type of jobs offered to a students after graduation. All these variables were used as my knowledge base to determine how well the school was doing. What was of ultimate importance was how successful students were after graduation. From the information I received, I was able to make appropriate changes.

The same principles of review and assessment apply to everything in life, including sixth sense development. With so much effort being put toward your development, it makes sense to monitor and access where you are. Your assessments also help to systematically focus your thinking on goals; and therefore, where you want to devote your efforts more efficiently over the next several months.

Zero In

We are now at the last letter, Z, for "zeroing in," our final tool in the guide to develop the sixth sense. "Zeroing in" means being deliberate and consciously choosing which-ever sense or senses you wish to develop on a higher level. Once you zero in on the sense you wish to develop, you may wish to use a certain number of sixth sense tools on a consistent basis and add others for a fresh perspective.

Zero In On a Sense

When choosing which sense or senses to develop, begin by taking time to think about what type of third dimension communication works best for you. For example, you could ask yourself, "Am I a more visual person?" "Am I a more in-tuitive person?" "Would I be more relaxed and receptive to using only gazing to ask for answers to my questions?" Only you can decide which of your senses is the strongest, the one on which to zero in.

You can work on your sixth sense development intensely and to the exclusion of other hobbies and interests, or you can just choose to zero in on your sixth sense development by being constantly aware of the energy around you. Everyone is different, so my advice is that if you are truly serious about sixth sense development, you should zero in on the sense or senses that interest you the most. Concentrate on developing the sense (or senses) until you have confidence in and trust your abilities.

Although choosing which sense or senses to develop is your choice, I have often found that directing one's efforts on developing only one higher sense to the exclusion of others makes for more directed and proficient sixth sense development. In addition, zeroing in on one sense boosts confidence and trust in knowing received messages are real, and not figments of the imagination. I have also found that concentrating on one sense results in more skillful and faster sixth sense development.

When you focus on one higher sense, you perfect your method of receiving messages and your method of interpreting them. The receipt and the interpretation of messages are equally important. What good is receiving a symbol in response to your question if it makes no sense to you or you come away with a totally different meaning than what was intended? Since you're focusing on one sense, all efforts, perception, and awareness are perceived through that one sense, making you a master of that one communication method. Developing your sixth sense is like everything else in life—if you're a specialist, you master what you do. When you dabble in lots of things, your concentration is less directed, even scattered.

Opening Peripheral Senses

When zeroing in on one sense, another sense may become peripherally heightened without any effort. It is interesting to note that sometimes when a person concentrates, for example, on the sense of higher sight, the sense of hearing may open even more than higher sight. This occurs when focusing on higher sight, the guard surrounding the auditory sense is down, allowing meaningful audio communication to be received. I refer to this phenomenon as "opening the peripheral senses." When the peripheral senses are opened, lots of sixth sense overlap occurs and many of the messages received are unsolicited, being more believable and useful to the recipient.

Zero In On a Tool

Once you decide which sense to develop, you may wish to focus on primary tools to aid your development. For example, let's say you'd like to develop your intuition. If you focus on the intuition as a sixth sense choice, the tools you may choose for its development might be awareness, breathing, and incorporating stones or crystals. Of course, you may add any others for variety.

Remember that as with anything else, sixth sense development can become routine. Don't let that happen. Although great for constancy, don't let the routine of sixth sense development become monotonous. If you feel dullness in your development, incorporate other tools—a new found understanding will emerge.

Some people have been known to intensely work on their sixth sense development for years, and then for some reason or none at all, they stop. Many years later, they may resume their interest with a very short learning curve and with many quick, positive results. They have quick, positive results because they already have the fundamental tools for sixth sense development. When people abandon their sixth sense development, it may be because the timing isn't right, like not being able to give the development the proper dedication and mental focus. Ultimately, everyone must do what's right for their life, in their own way, and at their own pace. However, I certainly hope you take the time to develop this very important part of your life. There are no negatives to having heightened senses—only a better, more fulfilling life.

Part III
Conclusion

You are a multifaceted being with unlimited potential. Take that potential, combine it with your divinely inspired uniqueness, and empower yourself to grow and advance your sixth sense abilities. Try to make a habit of spending quiet time looking inward. Discover your inner strengths, talents, and gifts. Nourish and develop those gifts with love and determination because by doing so, you will knock down barriers, unlock your senses, and ultimately open your life to all kinds of wonderful experiences.

I've spent my lifetime focusing on my passion, developing the sixth sense. I bring that same spirit to all I do, including my job as an attorney. My office bustles with people from morning 'til night. The phone rings constantly with questions and problems that need to be immediately remedied. Most times, the person on the other end of the phone is very emotional about whatever situation in which they find themselves. I love helping people with my knowledge and making a positive difference in their lives. I've brought that same passion to the writing of this book.

Whether you are new to sixth sense development or an expert in its applications, I suggest you read and re-read the concepts presented. Spend time thinking about all the tools and their applications to your life. Take any, some, or all of the tools and use them as your personal guide to help open the door to the higher senses. As you use the tools presented, expand on them and add your own. Practice your sixth sense skills consistently and deliberately. No matter how busy you are, make sure sixth sense development is a priority in your schedule. Maintain a holistic view of the body, mind, and spirit and the place each has in your sixth sense advancement. Feel gratitude for all the help you receive from the powerful, wise, and loving universal consciousness. It's up to you to determine how far you wish to make this work for you.

Be sure to maintain the view that everything is energy. Consistently maintain detailed records of your sixth sense progress and never doubt yourself in the various stages of your development. Don't get discouraged if progress doesn't occur as quickly as you think it should. Above all, never let anyone—especially yourself—discourage your development.

Along with the twenty-six tools to heighten the senses are three additional bits of advice I want you to follow to help advance your senses in extraordinary ways.

First, begin a study group with like-minded people. Including at least one other person in your sixth sense studies will help you remain on track with your development. With other people involved, your sixth sense development will become routine without becoming monotonous. The support from others, constant banter, and exchange of information will be invaluable.

I also suggest you read and re-read the biographies or autobiographies of famous intuitives. I am not suggesting any "how to" books, but the books that set forth the intimate details of their lives. By reading their life stories, you will find comfort in the difficulties these advanced spiritual beings experienced in coming to terms with their mystical talents. Walk with them as their gifts blossom and flourish. Watch as their character strengthens before your eyes as they embrace their sixth sense abilities. Feel their personal transformation as they surrender to forces greater than themselves. Experience the trust and confidence they gained throughout the years in their abilities. Grow in spirit with them as they mature in the development of their gift. Share their spirit of selflessness as they tirelessly devote their lives to helping others. Above all, make their highly tuned sensitivity to energy your incentive to keep you on track and focused when working with the A-Z tools.

The following are just some of whom I consider great intuitives and whose books I've read more than once for my own guidance and inspiration. Every time you read these books, you'll get more and more out of them for your own life's lessons. Each book is about a remarkable person who has a remarkable life story to tell. Although in most cases either they or someone else has written more than one book about their life, the one noted is the one with the most relevance for our purposes. As an added benefit, tucked within the pages is insight into the methods and rituals these great teachers relied on to fire up their sixth sense. I've listed the books in a section at the back, "Recommended Reading."

My last bit of advice is this—just because you are at the end of this book does not mean you are on your own. The book and its teachings and examples remain with you as your teacher, guide, and support system. Read, re-read, and refer to this book often. Make this book your life-long sixth sense development guide and you will notice how quickly you feel empowered in mind, body, and spirit. When you do, enjoy the instances of newness and abundance that begin to unfold simply for heightening your senses.